Bermuda's Essential Travel Guide

Discover the best Hotels,Beaches,malls and night parties for your trip to Bermuda

Table of Contents

Copyright

Introduction

I want to thank and congratulate you for downloading the book, *"Bermuda's Essential Travel Guide."*

In this book, you will discover the best hotels, malls, and beaches for your Bermuda trip. Bermuda has been dubbed as a paradise, and in this book, you will see walk-throughs and tips that will help you prepare and make the most out of your trip.

The first chapter covers a quick overview of Bermuda including its history, geography and people so you know what to expect when you get there, not just in terms of things-to-do but also in terms of how well you will be received by the locals.

Every savvy traveller understands the importance of that knowing a destination's peak and off peak seasons, which is why Chapter 2 touches briefly on the best times to visit Bermuda. If you intend to travel during peak season, you might want to know about them as it could be pretty crowded. However, there is also information on the different months in a year where certain festivals and parades take place. After all, you might want to plan your itineraries around said events. The second chapter will enable you to get the essentials for your Bermuda trip ready.

Nonetheless, even if you aren't targeting a specific event, you aren't likely to run out of things to engage in when you visit the islands. Chapter 7 has got you covered. It contains details on the best activities including operators to contact as well as suggestions on DIY-ing, especially when it comes to trail hiking and walking.

There is also information regarding tour operators, in case you need assistance and would want to make sure you maximize the time you can spend there by letting experts show you around the island. Some of these tours are covered in Chapter 10.

This book will also take you to the hotspots in Bermuda such as the best hotels and restaurants. They have been categorized based on price range and we have also included recommendations regarding nearby areas, and in the case of the restaurants, the menu items you must try.

With the information in this e-book, you'll get to book early to make sure you have a place to stay at since tourists from all over the world will visit too. By scheduling your trips depending on the season and planning your itinerary well, you may maximize your time and money.

Let this book be your ultimate guide when traveling to Bermuda. Enjoy!

Chapter 1. Bermuda: History, Culture and People

Good on you for considering Bermuda as your next travel destination! It is indeed a breathtaking place where you can be one with nature and enjoy much deserved rest and relaxation.

History

The earliest inhabitant known to have "accidentally" reached Bermuda was a sea captain from Spain by the name of Juan de Bermudez. That was way back in 1503, and soon after, the area he discovered was instantly named after him – Bermuda. The landmass was uninhabited so he quickly sent word to Spain about this discovery.

According to Spanish records, Señor Capitan Bermudez visited the island twice but never had a chance to dock his ship. What he managed to do was to draw a map and then send it back to Spain to be recognized. Spain claimed the area and added it to the list of islands owned by the Spanish Empire.

Front Street, Hamilton, Bermuda, before there was a railway| Source: http://www.bermudarailway.net/then/history/files/front-lb.jpg

In the 1600s, English colony led by Admiral Sir George Somers finally set foot on Bermuda. He was born in the early 1500s but died a year after he discovered the island. The island was uninhabited but food was bountiful. The British soon claimed ownership Somers' Isles and sent the first British settlers in 1612.

Geography

Somers' Isles came to be known as The Bermuda Islands or Bermuda. It may be a far travel from the United Kingdom since it is a thousand miles south of Miami, Florida but it is a UK territory.

When Bermuda came to be a booming region for trade, it was legally divided into municipalities and parishes. The nine parishes are Pembroke, Hamilton, Smith's, Warwick, Southampton, Paget, St. George's, Sandy's and Devonshire. The municipalities that were incorporated later on were named as Hamilton City and St. George's town.

Bermuda is not a big island but rather, made up of 138 islets. To group the islets in one sovereign government, the largest islet was declared as the capital. It came to be known as City of Hamilton. The form of government in the Bermuda Islands is Parliamentary as headed by HM Queen Elizabeth II. Governor George Fergusson has acted as Governor in 2012 and Head of the Government led by Premier Michael Dunkley in 2014.

Demographics

Home to the early English settlers, Bermuda has a population of 1,500 people who came from America, Canada, Portugal and West Indies. In 2010, the Bermuda Census reported a booming number of 64,237 inhabitants. Bermuda is home to blacks, whites, Asians and other nationalities. These inhabitants were migrants or people born within the lineage of the early settlers.

Personality-wise, Bermudians are more American than British. One trait that is particularly remarkable is their being on-time. In addition, what makes them British is the way they follow proper etiquette. They value protocol and manners, follow laws and value their implementation. Yes, Bermudians are indeed hospitable but if you are rude or show any kind of bad behavior, you may bring out the worst in them. The territory has a 99% literacy rate.

Aside from the mentioned traits, Bermudians are known for their charm and being a gracious host. In fact, this trait may stem from the island's main source of trade – fishing, farming and whaling and yachting. Tourists who have visited the island kept coming back for these splendid memories.

It is common to the locals to strike a conversation with tourists. Bermudians are articulate and educated since there are numerous schools and universities in the area. Since the culture and tradition is mainly British, as an American tourist, you need to be acquainted on the standard time format they follow. In the U.S., the month goes ahead of the day and year. In Bermuda, the format is day, month, and year.

The language or dialect being used is English with a telltale British accent. If they were to write down certain words, do not be surprised that their spelling is very British. For example, a savory meal is written as "savoury meal." Their favorite food is spelled as "favourite." You will eventually get the hang of the British side of Bermudians as you spend time in their company.

According to the 2012 projection on population, Bermuda will grow by 64,867. This was based on 2010 population census that the island had 64,237 inhabitants. With this in mind, the cost of living in this island makes it difficult for people with a low budget. Bermudians rely heavily on the bulk of tourists visiting the area.

Chapter 2. Starter Guide For A Trip To Bermuda

Every tourist should know the real story behind the places they visit. Since you have embarked on a journey, you need to know the ins and outs - figuratively and literally -- of this beautiful place.

Travel Documents and Requirements

Even if Bermuda is only a 2 hour plane ride from LAX, you need to present a valid passport. Thank the Department of Immigration in Bermuda for changing their visa requirements in 2014. However, this does not give you instant access to Bermuda since you need to make sure that you have a return ticket to show immigration. Should you hop on to other countries after your vacation in Bermuda, you need to present an eTicket showing your connecting flight. Being in an area where there is a massive turnout of visitors, safety may not always be a guarantee. Some visitors disrupt the peace.

Keep in mind that you have to declare your place of origin, length of stay in Bermuda, passport details and the date of your departure.

Peak seasons

The off-peak season is during the winter season, which is usually around November until February (some would say March is still a bit cold though). During this time, the temperature fluctuates from the low 60s to the high 60s. You might want to visit the area during this time if you're looking to avoid the crowd. You will, however, want to wear jackets especially during early morning and nighttime.

May to October is Bermuda's beach season, with temperatures ranging from the high 60s to the mid-80s. You will want to visit during this time if you're looking to enjoy sunbathing and beach life. However, many hotels, especially the luxury ones, charge a premium for accommodations during this period. You'll want to book hotel rooms several months ahead of time if you want to save money.

The best months to visit for those who are on a budget is March and April. It's that sweet period between off-season and beach season. The ocean might still be a bit cool, especially during March, but the festive atmosphere is turned way up during these two months. On Easter Sunday, islanders would do to Horseshoe bay and bring beautiful homemade kites.

Emergency numbers

For you to enjoy your stay in Bermuda, you need to settle down first and get to know some safety precautions.

- Keep the Bermudian police number handy at all times. You can reach them at 1 (441) 299-4431; in case of emergency, the number to call is still 911.
- For any medical requirements do contact King Edward Memorial Hospital at 1 (441) 236-2345.

- The U.S. Consulate may be reached during the day from 8 until 4:30pm at 1 (441) 295-1342 and 1 (441) 335-3828 at nightfall.

Custom Fees

Speaking of Custom responsibilities, Bermuda is an isolated place. Keep in mind that the government's source of income is quite limited. Tourism is their bread and butter so do not create havoc when asked for fees for the things you brought in to their island. Traveling to Bermuda is not expensive since every tourist is given a Duty Free Allowance. This allowance allows you to bring a certain amount of valuables in as well as bring home valuables without paying too much.

Here are some of the things that are exempt from duty (go over it, you pay)

Product	Volume	Customs Tariff (in Excess)
Spirits (vodka, rum, whisky, gin)	1 liter	$10.63/liter
Cigarettes	1 carton	$44.00/carton
Cigars	50 pieces	-
Medications (personal)	-	-
Infant food	-	-
Milk, curd, cheese, honey	-	5% of retail price (RP)
Meat (personal consumption)	-	5% RP (20 lbs. /person)
Seafood (personal consumption)	-	10% RP (20 lbs. /person)
Vegetables (personal consumption)	-	5% RP (20 lbs. /person)
Coffee (personal consumption)	-	5% RP (20 lbs. /person)
Disposable batteries (gadgets)	-	33.5% RP

What to do when you lose your passport

It is important to get the address and telephone number of your embassy. Do this before you even leave for a trip. However, if you did lose your passport and you have yet to do a courtesy call with your embassy, call them as soon as possible. Advise the office of the consul of your whereabouts. You will need this to allow them to track and get hold of you for further notices. If there is an uprising of militant groups in the country, get in touch with any of the military bases nearby.

If by any chance your hotel insists that you leave your passport with them for safekeeping, do not panic. It is a custom and at the same time, a guarantee that you are not going to sneak out of the hotel premises without paying. For instance, it you are in Italy, most hotels require that you leave your passport. If you are uncomfortable leaving your passport with them, carry a certified true copy of your passport together with a photocopy as well. The hotel can accept that instead of your real travel documents.

Losing a passport is difficult in so many ways. Passports are your ticket to going in and out of a foreign country and losing them is downright challenging. Well, there are ways for you to acquire a new passport during your foreign country trip. You need to submit the requirements at the US embassy:

- Form DS-11 Passport application
- DS-64
- Proof of primary identification and US Citizenship
- Police report stating that the passport was lost or stolen

- Passport photo

For expedition of your passport, make sure to have a copy of your itinerary since it will show the date you left the US and the date you arrived at your destination. Make sure you take have several photocopies of your passport, and itinerary.

The embassy will require you to pay fees to produce a new passport. Make sure that you pay in US dollars or local currency notes. Keep in mind that when pay for the fees, the US embassy does not accept Traveler's check, personal check, debit and credit cards.

After submitting your requirements, wait for about 24 hours for the embassy to issue a temporary passport. In Bermuda, you will be issued with temporary passports. Please remember that the validity of the passports is six months. You need replace and renew your 10-year valid passport the moment you return from your trip.

A tourist is subject to the legal system of the region where he committed the crime. Early as now, you need to know that bootlegs or illegal products are also available in Bermuda. It is of course against the law to purchase such and returning back home might put you in danger. Keep in mind that your passport is not a shield to anything that will protect you from this unsolicited danger.

General Safety Tips

There arc instances when tourists make it so easy to get themselves apprehended by the local police in a foreign country. Keep the following tips in mind:

- Safeguard your things and do not leave them scattered around.
- Take advantage of the hotel safes if they are available in your room.
- Nightlife in Bermuda is safer when you walk along well lit roads and look after your drinks on the table. However, try to refrain from loitering around Hamilton which can be found at the Dundonald Street.
- Rental vehicles are provided but secure your items in its carriers; bring a lock and key or request for it.
- Drivers in Bermuda follow left-hand driving with a driving speed of 22mph.
- When in Bermuda, it is advisable to always walk on the right side of the streets.
- Bermuda was built with narrow walkways and minimal sidewalks; follow the global pedestrian rule on stopping, looking and listening before crossing streets.

It is a standard protocol that you look after your things. However, when you visit Bermuda, according to the Bermuda Police Service Report in September 2014, incidents of burglary have impressively decreased. Secure your belongings at all times. To keep guests safe, police watch is 24/7 and is more than helpful to accommodate your questions, complaints or plea of help.

Protecting yourself from sickness

Due to the inclement weather in Bermuda, you need to make sure that your immune system is strong. Here are eight vaccine shots on viruses or diseases that most doctors require. It is advisable to have these shots updated prior to your trip:

- Typhoid
- Hepatitis
- Tuberculosis
- Hepatitis B
- Rabies
- Tetanus
- Polio
- Diphtheria

Should you plan to visit Bermuda or nearby Caribbean islands, you need vaccine shots against Malaria. If you often visit other countries within a span of 6 months to a year, keep in mind that these vaccines are still up to date.

The following vaccines are good if you had them recently - Typhoid lasts for 3 years, Hepatitis for 12 months, Polio and Tetanus for 10 years. While you are scheduling for your vaccines, invest in a good insurance carrier as well. You will need medical insurance especially if you are planning an overseas trip. Remember that no one can control accidents from happening. If you are insured then it is time to check your coverage if overseas trips are covered.

What to Pack for your Trip To Bermuda

Organize your carry-on bag by using zip-lock bags. If you are bringing cables for your gadgets, purchase garden wires to avoid tangles and for easy access.

- Face spritzer to keep skin hydrated (plain water is accepted in spritz bottles since pressurized cans are detrimental to the plane and passenger's safety once it goes airborne)
- Eye mask (must-have to prevent jet lag or aid relaxation)
- Shades (must-have when you disembark after passing the international date line)
- Short blanket (if the plane provides, make sure they are sealed if not then use your own)
- Compression socks (prevents swollen feet)
- Neck pillow (the plane provides but if it not sealed in plastic, decline and do not use inflatable pillows for the pressure in the cabin could burst it)
- Earplugs or noise-cancellation headphones (suitable for in-flight noisy passengers)
- Power bank for gadgets (iPod, iPad, iPhone)
- Belt bag (wear this under your shirt or blouse to secure money, passport, gum and breath mints)
- Sanitizing wipes
- Eye drops
- Nasal sprays (pressurized cabin air is dense and dry)
- Over-the-counter medicines (Benadryl will make you drowsy and sleepy so give in and rest)
- Plastic water bottle (airports prohibit these containers but it can be purchased inside once you pass through the security check)

- Lotion, hand cream, lip balm, toiletries, vapor rub to mask odor, deodorant stick, tampons

Clothes Appropriate For Bermudian Weather

The weather in Bermuda is a relief if you are from the cooler East Coast. From May until the middle of October, temperatures begin to rise. You will feel at home is you are from the warmer West Coast and visit during the hottest months from June until November. During these months it is advisable to pack cotton-made clothes and linens.

The weather is really warm but some rains may happen when a tropical storm brushes near. There are umbrellas sold everywhere since pointy rain gears are often confiscated in airports. However, the wind gusts in Bermuda are quite strong which in turn, can overturn an umbrella. Disposable rain gears such as rain coats and ponchos are advisable.

Dress code

Bermuda locals are highly influenced by their British traditions. Having said this, locals are conservative are not accustomed to vulgarity and nudity. It is a common understanding among tourists that Bermuda's beaches do not allow nudity.

Keep it cool but fashionable. Casual wear is the standard. Pair shorts with button-down shirts. Sneakers are common but, if you must visit the high-end hotels and clubs, your sneakers stay in the hotel. Ladies and gentlemen both wear relaxed outfits except when clubbing at posh joints. However, if you plan to go clubbing with your friends, it is safe to bring shorts dresses (for women) and slacks and collared-shirts for men.

Bring your leather shoes and high heels when you visit Bermuda. There are high-end places that require proper attire. Nevertheless, do pack your flip flops especially if you are going to the beach. Your kids will do fine in their sneakers and sandals.

Keep a low profile when visiting a foreign country. Even if you know that it is a safe place to spend your time there, you cannot disregard the risks of looking ultra-rich.

Safeguard your belongings. If you have a habit of storing your wallet or mobile phone at the back of your jeans or shorts, leave that habit at home. Carry the bare minimum when it comes to valuables.

Depending on the season, you might need a light jacket, or a lot of summer dresses and clothing.

Chapter 3. Getting to Bermuda

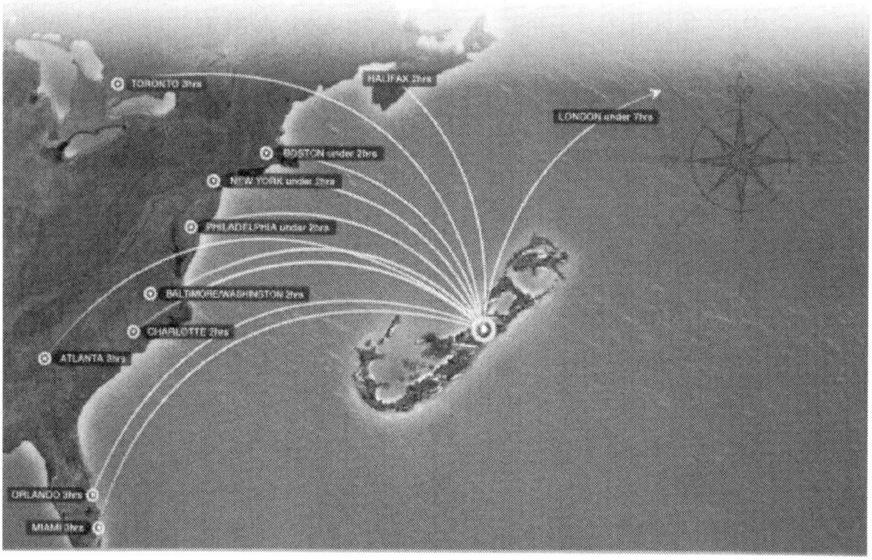

Image Source: Bermuda-online.org

By Air

The Bermuda International Airport (BDA) is at Kindley Field Rd., St. George's. The contact number is at 441/293-2470 and their website is Bermuda airport. Keep in mind that there are no rental cars in Bermuda as well as buses that stop to load in tourists and their luggage. The perfect mode of transportation is a minivan.

There are airlines that have daily, weekly, and seasonal flights to Bermuda. Here is a list of the airline companies you can get in touch with for a week of fun, sand and memories. The travel time usually takes 2 hours and 17 minutes. For illustration purposes, the airport for departure is at the JKF International Airport, New York. The airport for arrival is at the L.F. Wade International Airport (BDA).

American Airlines

If you are from Boston, New York or other airports in the US, this airline can bring you to Bermuda for $464. The returning airfare is the same.

Phone Number: 800-433-7300
Website: americanairlines

Delta Air Line

If you are from Boston, Atlanta, or New York, the airline can take you to Bermuda any day of the week day for $262. The returning airfare is the same.

Phone Number: 1-800-241-4141
Website: delta

United Airlines

If you are from Philadelphia, Boston, Atlanta, or New York, the airline can take you to Bermuda any day of the week day for $288. The returning airfare is the same.

Phone Number: 1-800-UNITED-1 (1-800-864-8331)
Website: united

JetBlue Airlines

If you are from Boston, or New York, the airline can take you to Bermuda any day of the week day for $128. The returning airfare is the same.

Phone Number: 1-800-JETBLUE (1-800-538-2583)
Website: JetBlue

In Bermuda, tourists who request for a taxi in the airport should leave 10 to 15% tip for the driver. For the Bermudians who help carry your luggage from the airport gates to the taxi, they are tipped at $1 per piece.

By Cruise Ships

Around 60% of the tourists who arrive in Bermuda are from cruise ships.

Bermuda is located south off the east coast of the United States. It's not exactly near continental US. Still, it is a popular tourist destination especially during Late Spring And Summer, when temperatures are around 80 degrees F. Crows flock to this sub-tropical island for its beautiful beaches, mild temperature, golf courses, and for water activities such as fishing and kayaking. Many cruise lines offer 5 day cruise packages, giving the passengers about 3 days to explore Bermuda and the surrounding islands, or to just relax.

It's easy to book a cruise. Just visit the cruise line's websites or its affiliates and indicate departure and arrival dates and preferred port of calls. Cruise ships dock on either Hamilton, King's Wharf, or St. George. Celebrity Summit and Royal Caribbean are two of the more popular operators.

Celebrity Summit has a smaller cruise ship which means that there is a smaller crowd and that the staff can manage and therefore offer consistent service. The operators put a lot of effort in providing decent food and wine offerings and the atmosphere is a bit subdued compared to what is expected of a cruise line. During peak seasons such as May until August, you may have to book a week in advance. The cruise line offers a 7-night and a 9-night cruise (other operators offer a 14-day Bermuda cruise, if that's what you're looking for). Rates range from $499 for interior accommodations to $2100 for a suite. Departure points include New York and Cape Liberty.

Royal Caribbean also has cruises to Bermuda. Their cruise ships are massive, featuring huge dance floors and multiple dining options ranging from Asian to Italian. There are also bars and a steakhouse on the ship. Entertainment includes aerial shows. Departure points include New York and Cape Liberty. A standard 5-night Bermuda cruise from Royal Caribbean is around $565.

Hiring a Travel Agency vs. DYI

You can still do all the flight booking, shuttle servicing and itinerary planning, especially with this e-book. Should you opt to acquire the services of a travel agency, make sure they are reputable.

You might actually end up saving money because agencies have the contacts that enable them to book tickets faster and at lower rates and get in touch with suppliers for shuttle services and budget hotels. Most travel agencies purchase tickets by bulk so it means you are getting a discounted price. These people know whom to call, when to do it and how much to settle for.

Ask for the list of big clients and suppliers that the travel agency is dealing with. This list is open to the public and should be available anytime. You can verify by giving some of the clients a call and asking if they are satisfied with the service.

Some people hesitate about hiring a travel agency because of the fees. It is that some agents charge extra fees for time and research rendered. However, these people get their commissions from the travel suppliers. So before you buy that $1,000 ticket to your desired destination, think again. Perhaps, a travel agency can look for a way to lower the fare.

Chapter 4. Getting Around

Tourists do not get to drive around the streets of Bermuda. There are laws that prohibit non-British nationals to use their driver's license even if it was intended for international purposes.

Tourists are advised to get a minivan to bring them to their chosen destinations. These taxis can carry four people and their entire luggage. These taxis are expensive but keep an eye on the flag-down rate. This rate is the fixed amount that is shown on the meter. $6.40 then for the first mile you pay $6. An additional $2 will be added for another mile. It is common knowledge that the farther you go, the higher your taxi fares are. It is advisable to always carry a map or make an itinerary on the places to go to. This will save you time and money.

Taxi/Minivan

Hourly to 3 hours rate: $50 - $85

Here, the driver will pick you up, bring you to your destination and bring you home.

Motorbikes (mopeds)

Rental rate (single rider): $48 (daily), $173 (5 days)

Rental rate (two riders): $53 (daily), $174 (4 days)

The payment scheme of the mopeds is via credit card. On top of the rental fee, you need to pay $30 for an insurance policy. You are insured for the duration of the rent.

Bicycles

21-speed mountain bike rental rate: $30 (daily), $65 (3 days)

A one-time insurance policy amounting to $15 is required. For an adventurous tourist, bikes are often suggested. However, Bermuda's land terrain is on an uphill and often times get muddy and slippery.

Oftentimes, tourists choose a day to visit the nearby sites in Bermuda and call it quits after an hour or two. Bear in mind that the roads in Bermuda are narrow and dimly-lit areas are quite alarming. One thing more, even bicycle riders follow left-hand driving.

Cruising along the old railways require that you bring your bicycle, horse or moped. There are several vehicles for hire. The rental fee is affordable depending on where you hire them from. As an example, if you decide to rent the bikes from hotel, they are priced at $30 a day. They come with locks and helmets for you to use.

Bus

Bus fare: $3/5 mi., $4.50 (beyond 5 miles)

There are different terminals for buses in Hamilton. The island has narrow streets where buses pass through 11 terminals to reach different destinations. Look for color coded markers such as the blue and pink poles. Keep in mind that the color coded markers have its specific bus routes. The pink coded bus stops are intended passengers going to Hamilton; the blue coded are those leaving Hamilton.

Always prepare an exact amount when you pay the bus driver. There is a fare box that does not accept bills. The bus driver will not stop just to open the fare box and give change to his passengers. To avoid hassle and the loss of money, there are also booklets you may purchase at the central bus terminal. The booklets have 15 tickets amounting to as low as $12 for a day to $45 for a week. Due to the size of island and the infrastructure, almost all buses pass through main thoroughfares at regular speed limits of 35 kph or roughly 21 mph.

It is also important to schedule your trips before or after the busy hours. Buses in Bermuda are out in the morning and evening since it is considered as the transportation of all working Bermudians. However, just like in any country, the rush hour can never be ignored if you have reservations too. Riding a bus is much better after the rush hours so you would not have to fall in line to long.

Trivia: Why are there no rental cars in Bermuda?

Bermuda is a highly developed area but they do not have cars for rent. They are exclusively for the use of Bermudian residents. The reason behind this is that the island is rather small so importing several vehicles will cause high road congestion. One thing more, the import duty to purchase a car in Bermuda is twice the amount in Canada, United States and Europe. Ownership of a vehicle is one per household. Imagine being stuck in traffic for the rest of day should 3 cars to a household be allowed. These privately-owned vehicles are smaller than the usual (hatchbacks, small sedans and the like) except for use of the Premier and the Governor of Bermuda. As tourists, it is always advisable to drive the available vehicles for rent such as the bikes, mopeds or take the public transport.

Ferry

Ferry fare: $4 (one-way)

You can go around Bermuda with your mopeds and bring it with you as you take a scenic route aboard the ferry. Take advantage of the connected transportation system in Bermuda since they allow the bus trip booklets to be used in the ferry.

For your reference, the ferries do not take cash as payment. And since these two modes of transportation are interconnected, paying with the exchange change is highly obliged. Just like bus terminals. The ferry ride followed a color coded trip. When you are going to the Dockyard and West end, take the blue route. If you are going to St. George's and Southampton, take the orange code. And if you are going to Warwick and Paget, take the Pink route.

Chapter 5. Hotels in Bermuda

Bermuda is where many people go to for some serious R and R so at the end of the day, you would want to sink in a comfortable bed inside a clean room. If you are looking for luxurious amenities, there are lavish resorts that can provide those. If you are on a rather tight budget and could forego certain indulgences, there are bed and breakfasts and other hotels that would be perfect. In this section, not only would you learn about what you can expect in terms of rates and amenities. You'd also get to know useful information such as how far it is from the airport, transportation options, and the nearby establishments you might want to check out.

Budget-friendly Options: Apartment Hotels and Bed and Breakfasts

Most of the suggestions are the more affordable options for hotels in Bermuda. Apartment hotels typically have an area where you can prepare your breakfast and snacks. Keep in mind that it is not customary for apartment hotel prices to be inclusive of meals. There are nearby restaurants you could visit for breakfast. Just as the more lavish hotels, these apartments have housekeeping so you do not have to worry about drying your clothes when you get wet from the beach.

The Sandpiper Apartments

Photo Credit: Google Map Bermuda

Address: South Shore Road, Warwick, Bermuda
Phone Number: +1 (441) 236-7093
Website: sandpiper

The Sandpiper Apartments is located in a residential neighborhood. The apartments are either studio or bedroom apartments. Each apartment has its own terrace and complete with amenities mentioned below. The staff can easily address to your needs because they speak English well. It is a kid-friendly hotel, but pets are not allowed.

It is located near the main road. It is a walking distance to the Swizzle Restaurant. There is also a nearby gas station and a small convenient store. It is also near a bus stop.

It is about 15 kilometers away from the L.F. Wade International Airport or a 30-minute ride, when using a Taxi service. A surfing and snorkeling beach is a ten-minute walk from the apartment.

Check in time is at 15:00 till midnight. Check out time is at noon.

Amenities: air condition, full kitchen, bathroom with shower, telephone, cable TV, BBQ pit, gas, outdoor pool, WiFi.

Room Rates: Cost per room varies depending on the season. If you are visiting Bermuda from November to March, they have a Studio apartment that is good for 2 guests. It costs $124. The Sandpiper has one room which is good for 3 people. An overnight stay amount to $175. If you are visiting Bermuda from April to October, their Studio apartments amount to $166. Their one room amounts to $209.

Clairfont Apartments

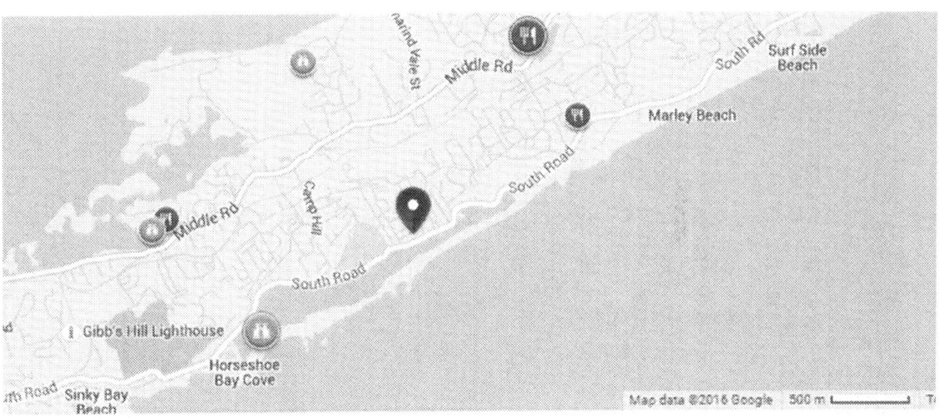

Photo Credit: Google Map Bermuda

Address: 6 Warwickshire Road, Bermuda
Phone Number: +1 (441) 238-3577
Website: clairfont

The Clairfont Apartment is near the Tucker's town. You can get to the town in just ten minutes through bus and taxi services. Guests can easily walk to the nearest beaches around the areas. The apartment is also near the Gib's lighthouse, where guests can enjoy a panoramic view of the beaches.

To get to the apartment, a shuttle service offered by the apartment may be availed. The apartment is approximately 15 minutes from the airport.

It is a kid-friendly apartment. Pets are not allowed though.

Check in time is at 15:00 to 23:00. Check out time is at 11:00.

Amenities: air condition, cable TV, WIFI internet, kitchen, telephone, outdoor pool, BBQ pit, full kitchen with refrigerator,

Additional Services: The management of the apartment also offers to arrange an exclusive taxi service for their guests. The management does not charge extra for this offer. Guests should only pay the taxi service.

Room Rates: The Clairfont has a single room with a large king-size bed, dining room and living room. The room costs $185. If your budget is lesser than the single room, better check in the Studio room for only $160 per night. The only difference is the bed size. Guests up to 3 people can comfortably stay there.

Dawkin's Manor

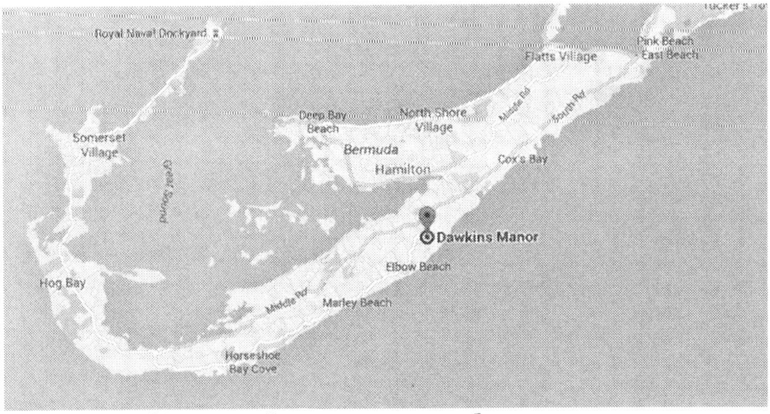

Photo Credit: Google Map Bermuda
Address: 29 St. Michael's Road, Paget Parish, Chelston, PG 04, Bermuda
Phone Number: +1 (441) 236-7419
Website: bermudacharm

The Dawkin's Manor is a 25 minute ride from the airport and is a 10 minute ride from Hamilton City. A five minute walk down south would lead you to Elbow Beach, where guests can enjoy diving, snorkeling, and canoeing.

The management also offers bike rentals. Guests can easily travel from the manor to the nearby Hamilton City and other nearby locations by biking.

The apartment is located in a business zone. A grocery store can be found within the block. Guests can visit a nearby golf course, about 3 kilometers from the manor. They also have easy access to the bus stop.

The rooms are soundproof. Thus, despite the busy traffic in the main road, the guest can still enjoy the tranquility in their rooms. The Dawkin's Manor is also ideal for honeymooners. They offer a bridal suite, which can be doubled as a honeymoon suite for the couples.

The place is great for kids. They have baby-sitting services and a children's playground. Pets are not allowed.

The management also offers safety deposit boxes, so the guests can wander the Bermuda without worrying about their precious things.

Check in time is at 14:00. Check out time is at 11:00.

Amenities: non-smoking/smoking rooms, air condition, cable TV, telephone, daily housekeeping. WIFI is available, but guests have to pay for it to avail it.

Room Rates: The Dawkin's has the 1-bedroom apartment, 2-bedroom apartment and 4-room apartment. Overnight stay costs from $106 - $305 depending on the room size. The manor allows 1 extra bed in each room, with additional charges. They also offer cribs for babies, but guests should make the necessary request during booking.

Paraquet Apartments

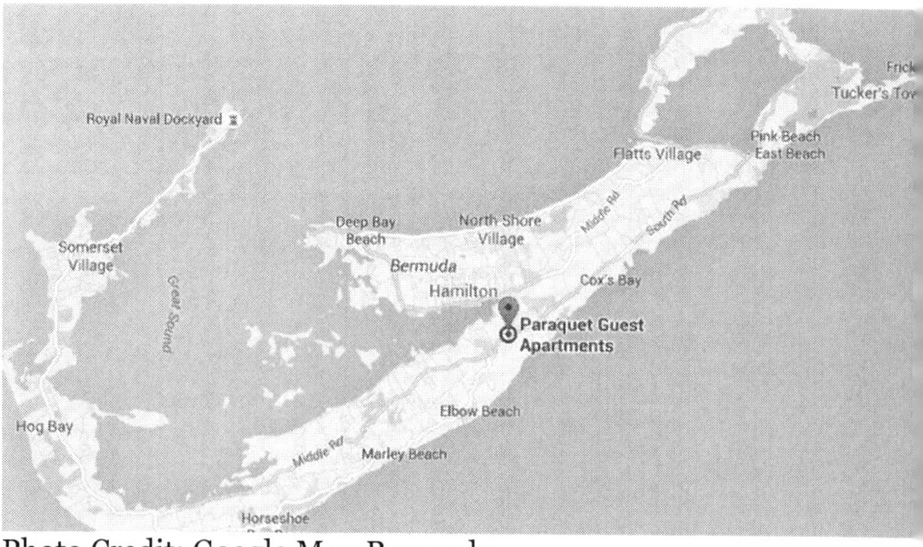

Photo Credit: Google Map Bermuda

Address: 72 South Shore Road, Paget, Bermuda
Phone Number: +1 (441) 236-5842
Website: paraquetapartments

The Paraquet Apartments is 15 miles from the airport. Guests can take a 10 minute ride to the Hamilton City from the property. The bus stop is just outside the gates. It is near the Dawkin's manor. All the activity center and beaches near the Dawkin's Manor can also be accessed from these apartments.

What makes the apartment standout is the Paraquet restaurant that is within the property. Guests can dine in the restaurant or order a take out.

Check in time starts at 11:00 and check out time is until 11:00, as well.

Amenities: air conditioning, WIFI internet, full bathrooms with showers, coffee maker, mini refrigerator and microwave. Some rooms are equipped with full functioning kitchen with oven.

Room Rates: All guest apartments and suites are non-smoking. The studio suites to 2-bedroom suites billet guests with prices ranging from $160 to $260 per night.

Robin's Nest Guest Apartment

Photo Credit: Google Map

Address: Vale Cl, Pembroke, Bermuda
Phone: +1(441)-292-4347

The Robin's Nest Guest Apartment is located 15 kilometers from the airport. It takes 30 minutes to get here via taxi services. It is a small property, which is why some travelers could not find it. The nearest bus is two minutes away from the property.

It is a ten minute ride to and from Hamilton City and a fifteen minute walk to the nearest beach.

Check in time starts at 13:00. Check out time is by noon the next day.

Amenities: air conditioning, free WIFI, full bathrooms with showers, kitchen equipped with refrigerator and microwave.

Room Rates: All guest apartments are non-smoking. The rooms have 1 bed for two people. No extra beds available. Price ranges from $80 to $150 per night.

Windsong Apartments

Photo Credit: Google Map

Address: 17A Berkeley Road, Pembroke Parish, Hamilton, Bermuda
Phone:+1 441-295-7221

The Windsong Apartment is a 30-minute ride from the L.A. Wade airport and a 6-minute walk to the Berkeley Institute. It is a small property with only 7 apartments. It is strategically located near a bus stop and just a 10-minute ride away from the Bermuda Aquarium and zoo.

Check in time is at 13:00. Check out time is until 11:00.

Amenities: Radio, Cable, TV, WIFI, Air-conditioning, Iron facilities, Shower, Bathtub, Free toiletries, Refrigerator, full self-catering kitchen equipped with kitchenware, stove-top with oven and toaster. Outside Pool

Room Rates: All apartments are non-smoking. The price range of the rooms is from $130 to $260 per night. The rooms can house 2 to 6 guests. No extra beds are offered.

Edgehill Manor Guest House

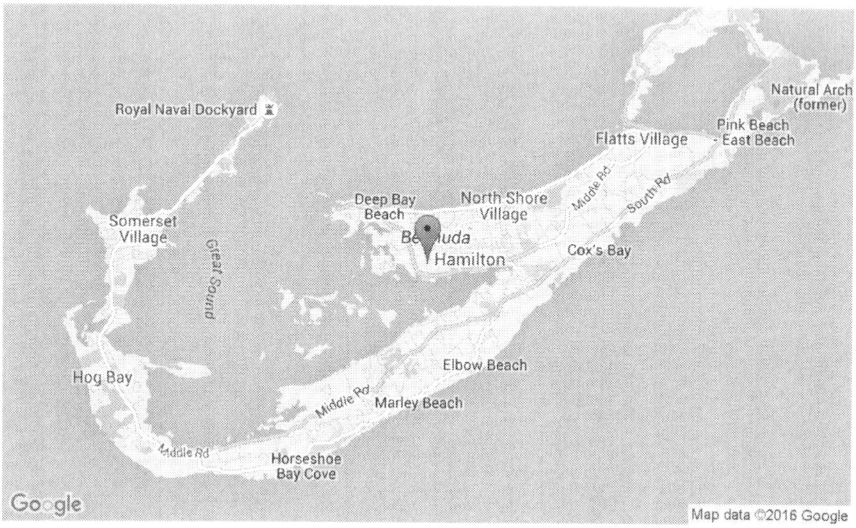

Picture Credit: Google Map

Address: 36 Rosemont Ave, Hamilton City, HM 06 Hamilton, Bermuda
Telephone No.: +1 (441)-295-7124

Website: www.edgehill.bm

The Edgehill Manor Guest House is a bed and breakfast with 14 rooms. The Hamilton Historic Center is a five-minute walk from the property. Guests can take a 15-minute walk to the Deep Bay beach to enjoy water sports and activities. The Royal Bermuda Yacht Club and Point Pleasant Park are within 2 miles from the guest house.

The staff can speak two languages, which are English and Filipino.

It is close to 2 supermarkets (The Miles and the Marketplace) and a liquor store. The supermarkets offer grocery deliveries for the guests of the manor.

Guests can dine in the Muse Restaurant, 500 meters away from the property. They can easily go shopping at the Hamilton downtown, which is a ten-minute walk from the property.

Amenities: TV with Cable, WIFI, a mini-fridge, microwave, toaster, sitting area in the room, bathroom complete with bathroom toiletries. Common areas include the barbecue facilities, outdoor pool, gardens and a designated smoking area.

Rooms: Price range of the rooms is from $210 to $450, this includes the free continental breakfast.

Mid-Range Beach Resorts

If you've saved up enough for some luxuries, and a better view, you might want to check out these beach resorts. Most of these are near the beach.

Grotto Bay Beach Resort

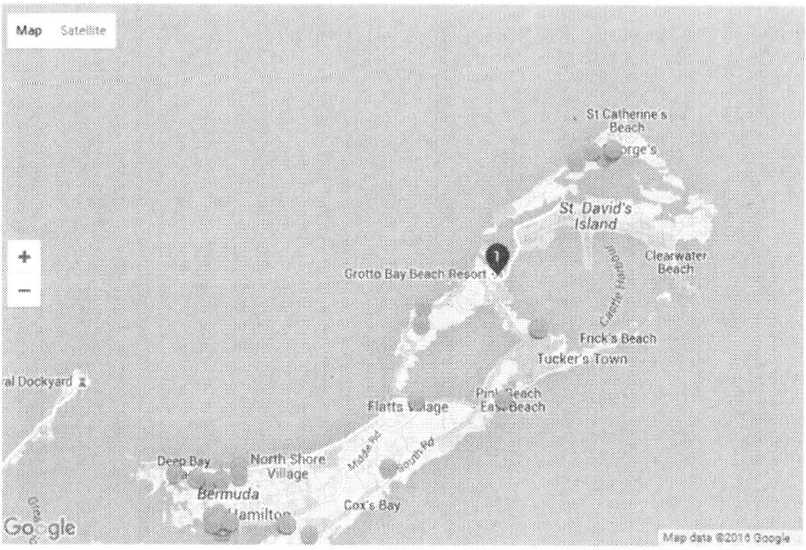

Photo Credit: Google Map Bermuda

Address: 11 Blue Hole Hill, Bailey's Bay, Tucker's Town, Bermuda
Phone Number: +1 (441) 293-8333
Website: grottobay

The Grotto Bay Beach Resort has a hotel with 200+ rooms. It has an outdoor pool, a private beach with water sports facilities. Guests can enjoy a day in their salon and spa, hot tubs, game room and playground for kids, tennis court and fitness center. Guests can also visit the Tucker's point golf course, which is four miles from the resort.

Guests can also dine in Hibiscus and Palm Courts Dining Rooms, the restaurants within the property that serve local and international food. It has a bar/club in the property, the Rum House Bar. Guest can shop for souvenir in the shop located within the property.

The resort is only 10 minutes away from the airport.

Check in time starts at 15:00 and Check out time is until 11:00.

Other Amenities: air-conditioning, cable TV, private toilet and bath, free WIFI and room service for each room. All the rooms have ocean views.

Room Rates: For an overnight stay at the Grotto Bay, you will only need $240. Breakfast is not inclusive of the bill.

The Reefs Resort and Club

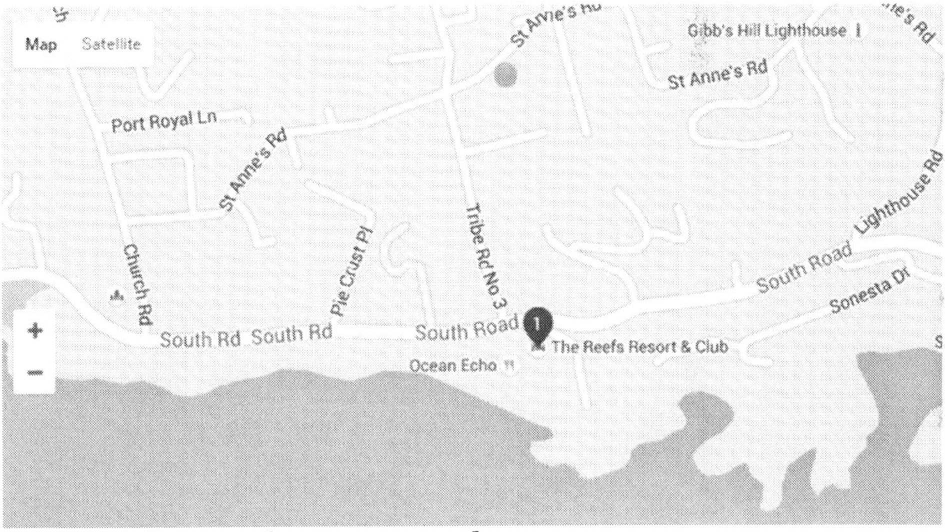

Photo Credit: Google Map Bermuda
Address: 56 South Road, SN 02, Bermuda
Phone Number: +1 (441) 238-0222
Website: thereefs

The Reefs Resort and Club is about 27 kilometers from the airport. Travelers may have to take a 40- minute taxi ride to the hotel. The Fairmont Southampton Golf Course is a 10-minute walk from the property. The Horseshoe Bay is a 15-minute walk from the resort.

The resort has a fitness center, tennis courts, hot tubs, private beach, massage parlor and spa. It features its own restaurant and bar.

Check in time starts at 15:00 and Check out time is until 11:00.

Amenities: daily housekeeping, complimentary WIFI, cable TV, mini-refrigerator, coffee maker, air-conditioning.

Room Rates: An overnight stay at The Reefs will amount to $217. Their 2 to 3-bedroom suite amounts to $450. Extra bed is charged for $50 dollars. Cribs or children's beds may be available, but should be confirmed by the management.

Famous activities available: Diving and snorkeling

Coco Reef Bermuda

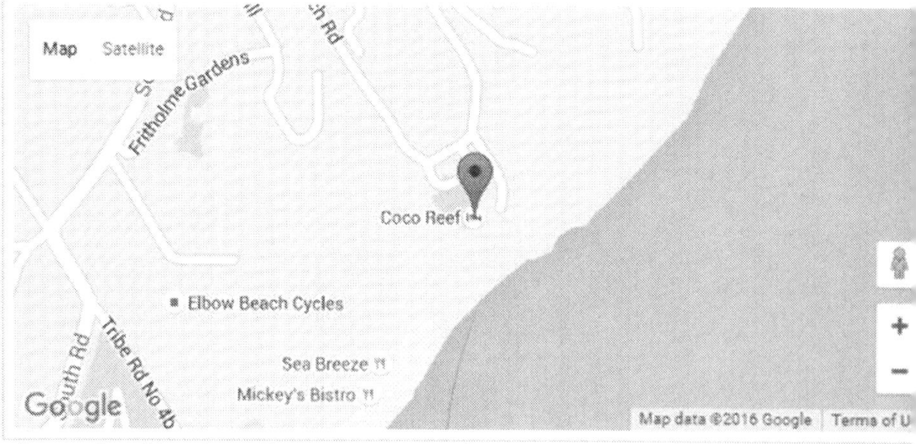

Photo Credit: Google Map Bermuda

Address: 3, Stonington Circle, South Shore Road, Paget Parish, Bermuda PG 04
Phone Number: +1 (441) 236-5416
Website: cocoreefbermuda

The Coco Reef Bermuda is a 15-minute ride from the airport. It has an outdoor pool and a common patio that is overlooking the ocean. It has its own private beach, souvenir shop, restaurant, bar and currency exchange.

It is a fifteen-minute walk to the Botanical Art Garden.

Check in time starts at 15:00 and Check out time is until 12:00.

Amenities: non-smoking rooms, refrigerator, complete toilet and bath, cable TV, telephone, WIFI. Common areas include the outdoor pool, patio, and the library.

Room Rates: An overnight stay at the Coco Reef will bring you to a $229 tab. This room can fit 4 people with their twin beds or 1 king sized bed. It accommodates children as well. Cribs are provided for children under two years of age. Extra child bed is charged at $14 to $100. Number of rooms:61

Luxury Hotels and Beach Clubs

If you are planning to spare no expense and treat yourself to a lavish Bermuda vacation, there are prime hotels in Bermuda where you will be pampered.

Hamilton Princess and Beach Club

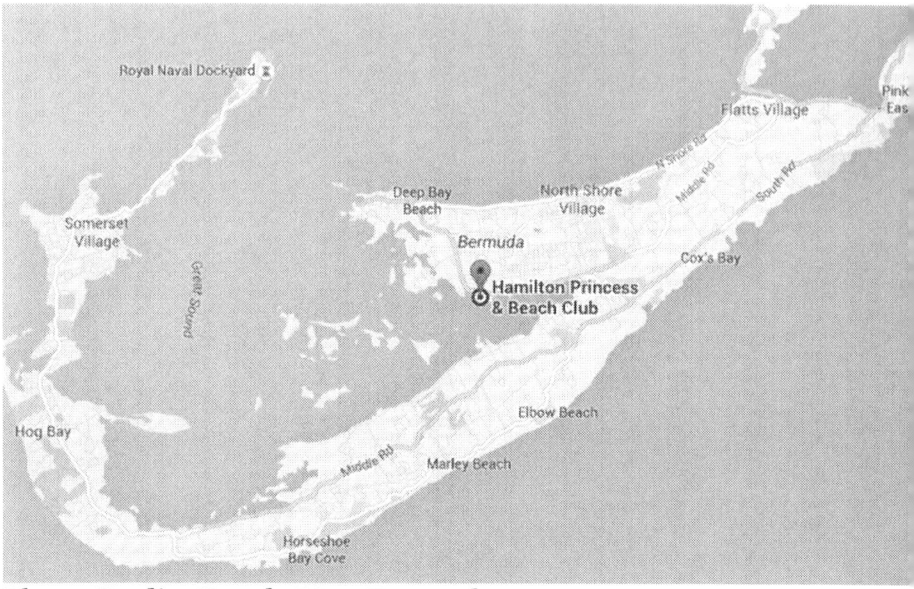

Photo Credit: Google Map Bermuda

Address: 76 Pitts Bay Road, HM08, Bermuda
Phone Number: +1 (441) 295-3000
Website: hamiltonprincess

The Hamilton Princess and Beach Club is a luxurious beach club at the heart of Hamilton City. It features a fresh water infinity pool with floating sun loungers. It has a private beach with on-site water sports facilities.

It has a kid-friendly environment and even offers extra child-bed and babysitting services. It also has facilities for people with disabilities.

It is a 30-minute ride from the L.A. Wade airport and a five-minute walk from and to Hamilton Downtown and harbor. Guests can choose to dine in the three restaurants available within the property and shop in the souvenir shops and luxury stores within the property.

Amenities: bathroom complete with tub, shower, towels, robes and other toiletries, Cable TV (Widescreen), WIFI, telephone, sitting/living area, alarm clock.

Other services offered: Airport shuttle, jitney ride to the beach, currency exchange, concierge services and ATM/Banking service.

Room Rates: Prices for an overnight stay range from $375 - $683. These rates depend on the type of room you choose – superior, deluxe to suite. Number of rooms: 410

Check in time starts at 15:00 and Check out time is until 12:00.

Royal Palms Hotel

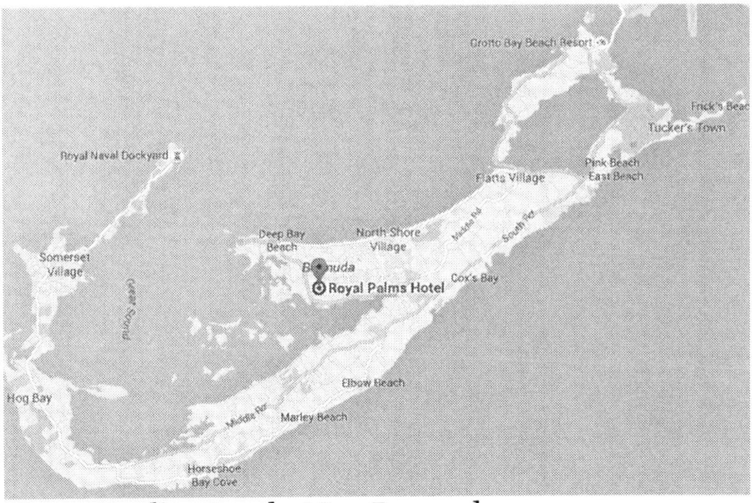

Photo Credit: Google Map Bermuda

Address: 24 Rosemont Avenue, 24 Rosemont Ave, HM06, Bermuda
Phone Number: +1 (441) 292-1854
Website: royalpalms

The Royal Palms Hotel is a coral-colored manor with 32 hotel rooms. It is about 500 meters away from the Harbor Marina. Guests can easily access water taxis to Hinson's Island. It is a five-minute walk to the Hamilton downtown.

Two restaurants can be found in the property, including the Ascot, which is popular to both locals and tourists. The property also has its own bar.

Free buffet breakfasts are offered to the guests on the common terrace.

Check in time starts at 13:00 and Check out time is until 11:30.

Amenities: WIFI internet, cable TV, DVD player and ipod dock, air conditioning, kitchenette, shower, working desk and living area.

Other services: Concierge service, babysitting services, and laundry services.

Activities offered: Horseback riding, diving and snorkeling.

Room Rates: During the winter, a superior room at the hotel amounts to $350 per night. The superior suite amounts to $370, and the deluxe at $445. During summer, a superior room amounts to $339 per night. The superior suite amounts to $415, and the deluxe room at $385. Cribs and extra bed can be availed for $30 to $50.

Elbow Beach Hotel Bermuda

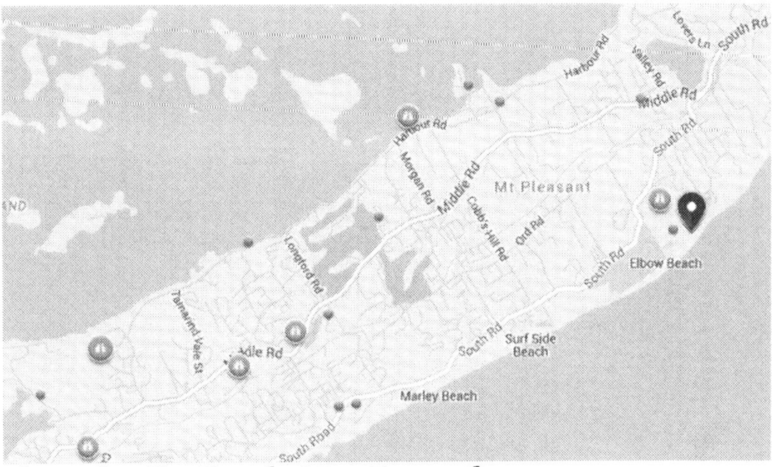

Photo Credit: Google Map Bermuda

Address: 60 South Shore Road, Paget Parish, PG 04, Bermuda
Phone Number: +1 (441) 236-3535
Website: elbowbeachbermuda

The Elbow Beach Bermuda is a luxurious 4-star hotel, a few meters away from the Elbow Beach. It is a 10-minutes ride to and from the Hamilton City and a twenty minute ride from the L.A. Wade airport.

It has five restaurants, a bar, a few on-site shops and a business center. It is one of the few hotels in Bermuda that allows guests to bring their pets.

Check in time starts at 15:00 and Check out time is until 11:00.

Amenities: TV, WIFI, telephone, Ipod dock, radio, bathroom with complete set of toiletries, living area, minibar, work desk, coffe maker, alarm clock, safe.

Common activity area: Billiards hall, Spa and Wellness center, library, tennis court, private beach area

Activities that can be arranged for the guests: snorkeling,diving, on- site water sports facilities.

Other services offered: shuttle services, babysitting and/or pet services, concierge, shoeshine, safety deposit box, and currency exchange.

Room Rates: An overnight stay in Elbow Beach's rooms amount to a minimum of $887. The prices will still go up depending on the season and room or suite sizes. Extra beds cost $50 dollars. Pet's cot or facility also charge the same amount.

Rosedon Hotel

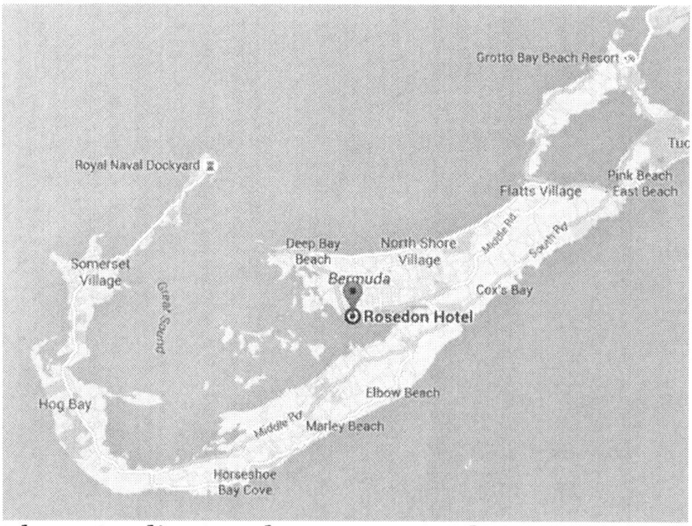

Photo Credit: Google Map Bermuda

Address: 61 Pitts Bay Road, Pembroke, Bermuda
Phone Number: +1 (441) 295-1640
Website: rosedon

The Rosedon Hotel is a three star hotel with 39 rooms. It is thirty minutes away from the L.A. Wade airport, 5-minute ride to the Elbow beach and a five minute walk to the Victoria Park. It is 500 meters away from Historical Society Museum.

The property has an in house restaurant, lounge and bar. But, guests can choose to dine at Robin Hood Pub & Restaurant or Barracuda Grill, which are about 5-minute walks from the property.

Check in time starts at 15:00 and Check out time is until 11:00.

Amenities: air-conditioning, cable TV, free WIFI, mini refrigerator, telephone, safe, coffee maker, bathroom with free toiletries, slippers and robes.

Common areas: Outside pool, Family rooms and common lounge

Activities that can be arranged by the management: Snorkeling and Diving

Room Rates: At Rosedon, guests can choose rooms such as standard to royal for as low as $300 to $450 a night.

Newstead Belmont Hills Golf Resort and Spa

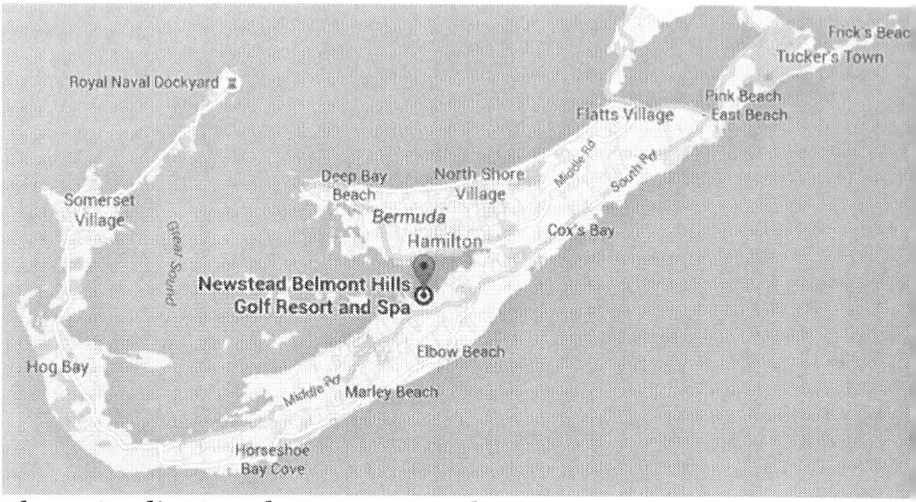

Photo Credit: Google Map Bermuda

Address: 27 Harbour Rd., PG 02 Bermuda
Phone Number: +1 (441) 238-6060
Website: newsteadbelmonthills

The Newstead Belmont Hills Golf Resort and Spa is overlooking the harbor. It has an 18-hole golf course on the property and on site restaurants. Guests can take a boat ride to the city of Hamilton, which is across the hotel. Guests can get a shuttle ride from the property to the south shore beaches (Elobw and Marley).

Check in time starts at 15:00 and Check out time is until 11:00.

Amenities: air-conditioning, cable TV, WIFI, mini refrigerator, living or seating area, coffee machines, alarm clocks.

Activity centers in the hotel: Tennis court, Ftness center, spa and wellness center, outdoor pools, and golf course. The golf course is three kilometers from the hotel and can be accessed through the hotel shuttle.

Other services offered: Shuttle services, boat rides, bicycle rentals, safety deposit box, concierge, child services.

Room Rates: Enjoy a $508 overnight stay at the Newstead Belmont and be treated like a god. The room rate for the latter is lower than their 2-bedroom price of $697. Their 3-bedroom suite is an eye-opener at $811 but wait till you get served on your every beck and call.

Rosewood Tucker's Point

Photo Credit: Google Map Bermuda

Address: 60 Tucker's Point Dr., Hamilton Parish, HS 02 Bermuda
Phone Number: +1 (441) 298-4000
Website: rosewoodtuckerspoint

The Rosewood Tucker's point is one of the most luxurious hotels in Bermuda. It is 15 minutes away from the international airport. Guests can simply take a five-minute walk to the Tuckers town.

Guests, however, may have to take a 20 minute ride to enjoy the night life and harbor lfe in Hamilton City.

Check in time starts at 15:00 and Check out time is until 11:00.

Amenities: Each room has a widescreen TV with cable, Ipod dock station, telephone, a work desk, safe, coffee maker, seating area, and a mini bar. The bathroom has a shower and a tub. Complimentary robes and slippers are given to guests along with free toiletries.

Common Activity areas: 4 large swimming pool, spa and wellness center, fitness center, a golf course, tennis courts, children's playground and a private beach area.

Activities that can be arranged for the guests by the management: diving, bike and scooter rentals,

Dining: The hotel has an on-site restaurant and bar. But, guests may avail of in-room dining.

Other services: Concierge services, babysitting services, on site gift and souvenir shops.

Room Rates: Choose from manors, manor suites, and villa rooms where guests are given lavish time and comfort. Prices for an overnight stay ranges from $425 to $3,500. Extra bed range from $40 to $75 dollars.

Cambridge Beaches Resort

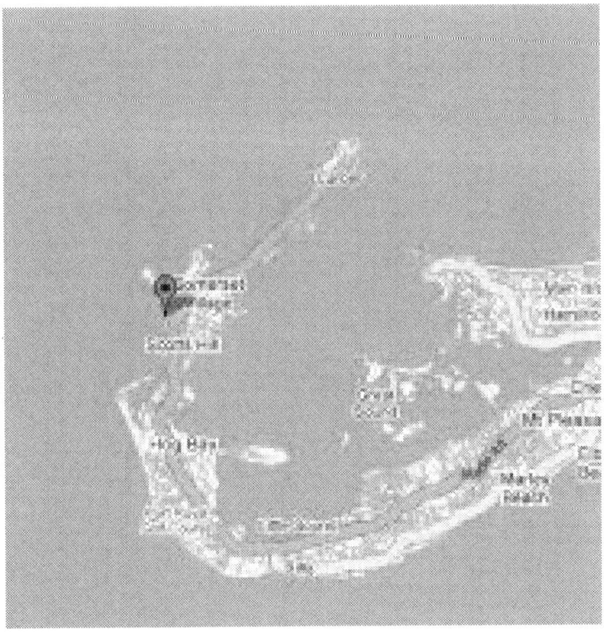

Picture Credit: Google Maps

Address: 30 Kings Point Road, Sandys Parish, MA02 Somerset, Bermuda
Telephone No.: +1(441)-234-0331
Website: cambridgebeaches.com

The Cambridge Beaches Resort is a luxurious hotel and resort that is exclusively for adults. The resort does not accept children, who are 13 years old and below. The main reason for the exclusivity is the fact that the cottages in the resort are more than 300 years old and the owners are afraid that children may damage them.

It is situated at the tail of Bermuda. It is about an hour away from L.A. Wade International Airport and 20-minutes away from Royal Navel Dockyard, where some good shops are located.

Guests can capture the beautiful sunset on the beach and enjoy the soothing gardens surrounding the resort.

Check in time starts at 15:00 and Check out time is until 11:00.

Amenities: Living area, work desk, TV, cable, Ipod dock station, safety deposit boxes, WIFI, refrigerator, electric kettle, bathtub and shower. Bath robes and slippers are provided. Toiletries are free.

Common Activity areas: Outdoor and indoor swimming pools, hot tubs, garden, patio, private beach area, massage and beauty parlors, spa and wellness center, fitness centers, tennis courts, golf course, sauna and library.

Activities that can be arranged for the guests by the management: diving, snorkelling, bicycle rentals, water sports and windsurfing.

Dining: The hotel has three on-site restaurants, a buffet, a fine dining and an *ala carte.* Free breakfasts are served in the room. The hotel has an on-site bar. Guest may also try the restaurants, grills, bars and cafes just outside the resort.

Other services: Concierge services, free shuttle services around the Somerset Village, the beaches and golf course, Airport shuttle with fee.

Rooms Rates: Rooms are usually for two adults. The price range is from $350 to $900. The prices do not include the 15% tax and the $15 service charge per person. Extra beds are not available.

Things to Remember when Looking for or Booking a Place to Stay in Bermuda

1. ***The apartments or self-catering accommodations are usually not available for walk-in bookings.*** These places have limited rooms. If you want to stay in these places, you should book in advance or at least two months before your vacation. Try to contact the apartments at around 11:00 in the morning (Atlantic Time Zone), which is the usual check-out time in most hotels in Bermuda. You may secure a room by doing so.

2. ***It is more expensive to bring your children.*** A vacation in Bermuda may be an experience for your children, but their accommodations may cost you extra fees or expenses. Most cheap apartment hotels and resorts are not kid-friendly. They do not provide extra beds for children. If you want your children to have a good vacation with you, you may have to book hotel resorts, which are more expensive.

3. ***Consider the goal for your trip***. Do you want to relax on the beach or do you want to explore? If you are one of those tourists who want to only roam around Bermuda and only need a place to sleep, you should consider booking some cheaper apartments or bed and breakfast. You may also try to find room for rents from the locals. Some locals rent out rooms in their houses to tourists. They are cheaper, but do not expect high quality amenities.

If you want to relax, enjoy the beach and the luxurious life, then you may have to stay at the beach resorts and luxurious hotels.

If you are looking for shopping and nightlife, you may consider staying at a hotel in Hamilton or Somerset Village, where most shopping centers are located and where the nightlife is terrific.

4. ***Be sure that the hotel or accommodation you avail suits your needs or expectation***. Most Bermuda hotels and accommodations observe a two day reservation fee policy. You have to pay the full amount of your reservation upon booking, if you are only staying for a day or two. If you

are availing the room for more than two days, you still have to pay for the first two days, upon booking. After the second day, you will be charged for the next two days. If you cancel your reservation before the end of the second day, you may not be refunded. So, you better make sure that the hotel is the place you want to stay during your vacation.

5. ***Do not bring your pets.*** Most hotels and other accommodations in Bermuda do not allow pets in their establishments. Establishments that allow pets, usually charge a rate, which is almost the same as an adult. They also require a lot of documents to prove that your pet is safe. You may not also bring your pets to tours and restaurants around Bermuda. So, to avoid the trouble, leave your pets at home.

Chapter 6. Bermuda Events And Festivals

All throughout the year, the Bermuda scene is throbbing with events and festivals. There are a lot of things to do in Bermuda. Here are some of the annual events in choice areas around Bermuda for which you may plan your itinerary for.

January

Bermuda Regional Bridge Tournament (23-29 January)

Where: 6 Southside Road, St. David's Island, St. George's

Phone Number (for reservation): +1 (441) 293-6083

Joining fee: $16/head

The locals run a card tournament called Bridge every last week of January. The games here are divided into different player levels consisting of beginners, intermediate and the experts. Tourists are welcome to join in the fun at the Fairmont Southampton Hotel. Joining is inclusive of tea in the afternoon, coffee in the evening, some snacks and drinks. This is event is an international game wherein you can meet other tourists as well as participants across the globe.

Bermuda Festival of the Performing Arts (15 January – 29 February)

If you are traveling to Bermuda around the months of January until February, why not join in the fun at the Performing Arts event? This 6-week festival happens in the evening around 5:30PM. Be thrilled with various performances from select performing art schools in Devonshire. They will provide the entertainment via music, comedy and drama. There are also international dances that will take place at the City Hall and Arts Center in Hamilton. The event is free for all.

February

Bermuda Heart & Soul (1 February onwards)

Phone Number (for reservation): +1 (441) 292-0023

Website: bta

Cultural activities are all over Bermuda for the month of February. There is the Golden Rendezvous where different hotels slash their rates exclusively for mature guests. This is one of the activities sponsored by the Bermuda Tourism Authority.

Initially, the celebrating Valentine's Day in Bermuda was limited to a couple of days. The BTA changed this provision and made February as the Love Month. Couples that visit Bermuda may avail discounted hotel rates, flight tickets and even resort accommodations.

March

Blue Sky Flights

Image Source: blueskyflights

Where: 6 Southside Road, St. David's Island, St. George's

Phone Number (for reservation): +1 (441) 293-6083

Time: 6AM to 11PM

Cost: $450/hour

Experience an hour in the air aboard a Cessna 172 Skyhawk plane. Tourists choose to have a first-hand experience to see shipwrecks that are still scattered around the fairways and reefs. A professional pilot will take care of the flight your aerial fieldtrip.

Afternoon Tea at Crown & Anchor

Address: 76 Pitts Bay Road, Pembroke, Hamilton, Bermuda, HM 08

Phone Number: + 1 (441) 295 - 3000

Website: hamiltonprincess

Cost: $48/head (inclusive of tea infusion, orange juice and coffee)

Bermuda is British by heart so by three in the afternoon, you can join other tourists and locals alike for the chance to sip tea in fine tea wares.

City Food Festival

Image Source: bernews

Bermuda has back to back activities for its locals and tourists alike. Every March, the towns prepare food competitions featuring top chefs in the area, wine tasting and food vendors scattered across Hamilton City. This month is every gourmand's heaven for 5 glorious days.

Zoom Around the Sound

Where: 40 North Shore Road, Flatts FL 04 Bermuda

Phone Number: +1 (441) 293-2727

Website: bamz

The Zoological Society of Bermuda knows how to pack laughter and countless memories with their 7.2 mile walk. There are other interesting races such as bicycling loop and running. This annual celebration's proceeds will be for the benefit of the Bermuda Aquarium, Museum and Zoo. If you are an animal lover, this event's for you!

Bermuda International Film Festival

Every country boasts of their film festivals and so does Bermuda! Enjoy films from award-winning directors and actors for 10 days. This event also includes mentoring for filmmaking and acting.

April

Bermuda Agricultural Show

Farming is important in Bermuda that is why during the month of April, they showcase their best crops in town to everyone. Every year, as much as 4,000 establishments join the exhibit to inform the crowd of their advocacies and charity work.

Bermuda Yoga Festival

Address: 11 Blue Hole Hill, Bailey's Bay, Tucker's Town, Bermuda

Phone Number: +1 (441) 293-8333

Website: grottobay

This event on the last day of April is a scene-stealer for people who wish to be one with nature, and themselves for inner peace. Better head on the Grotto Bay if you have checked in somewhere else on this day. They have yoga mats you can rent if you want to join in on the fun!

May

Bermuda Day (24 May)

Scheduled trips to Bermuda in the second week of May will allow you to experience Bermuda Day. There are parades along the roads of Hamilton as well as boats out at sea. This event usually starts around 1PM. This is a free event not to pass.

June

HM Queen Elizabeth II's Birthday Parade

Where: National Stadium, Devonshire

Address: 50 Stadium Cottage, Frog Lane, Devonshire DV01, Bermuda

Phone Number: +1 (441) 295-8085

Website: nationalsportscentre

Come join the Bermudians in wishing Her HM Queen Elizabeth well on her birthday. On this day, the Bermuda Regiment will be at the parade to salute the Queen together with the Bermuda Sea Cadets, Bermuda Police Service and the Bermuda Cadet Corps. Be there on or before 10AM since it will be televised back home!

This is your chance to see men in uniform riding on horses together with some members of the Royal Family. Well, their presence is still kept confidential for security purposes but it is sure that the Governor and Premier of Bermuda will begin the parade. This event is camera-worthy indeed for there is 41 Gun Royal Salute fired by the Royal Horse Artillery at 1252 hours. That is by 10:42AM in non-military language for you.

Heroes Weekend (17-20 June)

Majority of the tourists that visit Bermuda during this time will have an unforgettable time of the lives. This is a 4-day holiday where everyone can dance to soca music in several street parties.

July

Bermuda Fashion Festival (10-16 July)

Bermuda's Fashion Festival occurs on the second week of July. According to sources, in 2016 the Governor of Bermuda will recognize the main man behind the international group called Coach Inc. His name is Ian Bickley, a Bermudian and the president of this sassy and trendy accessory line. For more news about the Fashion Week, do log on to bermudafashionfestival.com. Tickets are out for sale as early as 1 March.

Non-Mariners Race (31 July)

Where: Somerset, Sandy's, Bermuda

Address: 8 Mangrove Bay Rd., Mangrove Bay, MA01

Bermuda is known for sandy beaches, good food, hospitable people and a beautiful marina. If you are travelling on the last week of July, there is an annual event where non-professional sailors can compete at noon time at the Mangrove Bay in Somerset.

August

There are several events happening around August. However, it is to be remembered that by this month, Bermuda has entered the hurricane season. There are still activities on the beachfront and marinas but as a tourist, it is recommended to stay indoors if you are already in Bermuda. Plan your vacation well around this month to ensure safety.

Gombey Festival (31 August)

Where: 2 Marsh Folly Road, Pembroke Parish, Bermuda

Phone Number: +1 (441) 292-0105

Website: communityandculture

Majority of the tourists crave for ethnic or folk dancing whenever they visit a foreign place. The last week in Bermuda is all about that – performers dance at the WER Jell Tennis Stadium dressed in their ethnic attire. According to the different travel guides, this event highlights on British, Caribbean, African and North American native music.

This is your chance to experience an educational and relaxing event on culture and people in Bermuda. Better eat a heavy lunch since the entertainment begins at 5:30PM. Do not worry about any joining fees since this festival is free of charge.

Bermuda Beach Tennis

When in Bermuda, you can get the beach action your body is craving for. Join spectators and international participants as they clamor for the top seed of the game. This event happens once a year at Horseshoe Bay Beach. It is sponsored by the International Tennis Federation (ITF). There is no joining fee to watch the games but it pays to buy island drinks to quench your thirst!

September

Bermuda Sand Sculpture

This is an annual competition where you can join in free; make beautiful sand designs under the hot Bermuda sand. There are prizes given for the most compelling sand castle design at the Horseshoe Bay Beach. The sand frenzy begins at 10AM until 4PM. The winners are chosen by 5PM. Hurry up and make memorable sand sculptures but don't forget the sunscreen for the sun gets fierce at this time.

November

Bermuda Tree Lighting Ceremony

Address: 17 Church St, Hamilton, Bermuda

Phone Number: +1 (441) 292-1234

Website: cityhall

Every year, Bermudians get busy preparing for the visit of Santa Claus. The event usually takes place at the Hamilton City Hall. Several locals gather around 5:30PM to await the ceremonial illumination of a large Christmas tree decked in glittering lights. Santa is the guest of honor together with the Deputy Mayor.

Bermuda Santa Clause Parade (end of November)

Address: 17 Church St, Hamilton, Bermuda

Phone Number: +1 (441) 292-1234

Website: cityhall

Along the streets of Hamilton, thousands of young kids eagerly wait for the coming of their much-awaited Santa Claus. The streets are decked with lights, surrounded by dancers, and tall clown-like looking mascots called Gombeys. The annual event is free! Be there before 5:30PM to get a good place to take pictures with the bearded guy.

December

Bermuda Christmas Boat Parade (12 December)

Image Source: gotobermuda

Head on to the Hamilton Harbour to take a glimpse of Santa! The harbour is at the west end tip of the island. You may reach Hamilton Harbour by getting a cab ride to the Royal Naval Dockyard. In Bermuda, the worldwide tradition is to see him roll down the street on his magical sleigh. In Bermuda, Santa takes his sleigh ride with a twist! See the bearded guy float on a magical water ensemble together with other well designed boats. This is one Christmas experience you can only see in Bermuda. Be near the shoreline by 4PM since the crowd will grow to an expected 20,000 participants by evening. This event is a must watch when you are traveling to Bermuda during the holiday seasons.

Chapter 7: Things To Do In Bermuda

Bermuda Island is pretty small so you are almost always within a few minutes' drive from the coast. That is why a lot of people visit the main islands and the surrounding islets for ocean-related activities like boating, kayaking, diving, and sailing. If you'd rather just lounge on the beach, you'll have no problem finding a good spot, so long as you visit during Bermuda's beach season which was discussed earlier in the travel guide. You can also just play golf; the golf scene has benefited from a much-needed revival back in 2002, and today, Bermuda is home to a number of golf courses.

Diving

You have probably heard of the Bermuda Triangle by now – an area in the Atlantic Ocean where hundreds of ships have perished. Many of the wrecks in the area are accessible to divers, which makes Bermuda one of the best destinations for scuba diving. You'll get to see ship wrecks of frigates and Civil War blockade runners. Some of these are located just 60 feet deep!

In addition, the waters in the area are also warmer even though it's well above the tropics, thanks to the Gulf Stream, which made it possible for coral reefs and other reef systems to thrive. These reef systems might not be as varied as those found in tropical areas such as the Caribbean; however, studies have shown that the reefs in the Bermuda era are some of the healthiest in the world.

Fishing in the Bermuda has been regulated well so fish stocks have fared better compared to those in the Caribbean. That is why Bermuda was able to maintain diversity in marine life, with over 400 species recorded. Diving in Bermuda waters will allow you to see these first-hand.

The waters are coldest during December to April so you'd have to gear up with a full wetsuit. However, during those months, Hotel rates are also significantly cheaper, and the waters are much clearer.

Dive rates are higher than standard US rates (around $90 for a one-tank dive and $130 for a two-tank dive). Contact reliable diving operators to get started.

Fantasea is a dive operator that caters primarily to cruise ship passengers but they do offer daily two-tank dives to qualified divers.

Blue Water Dives is a reputable operator which has been in the business for over 3 decades. They offer one and two dank dives, as well as PADI courses.

If you have booked rooms in the Fairmont Southampton or any place near the area, get in touch with Dive Bermuda. They are based on a beach nearby and they offer a range of PADI courses that would be appropriate for complete beginners and experienced divers. They also offer specialized courses such as Underwater Photography and Wreck Diving.

Boating and Sailing

There are many operators that allow you to rent small motor boats. The Boston Whaler is the best choice in boats because it is reliable and easy to maneuver. The boats' carrying capacity is usually about 4 to 6 people.

Reputable operators include Somerset Bridge Watersports, Blue Hole Water Sports, and Tucker's Point Dive, H2O Sports, and Watersports Centre. Your choice would ultimately depend on your location. For example, if you are located at Sandy's Parish, it's best to go for H2O Sports as they are based in the area. If you are located at Hamilton, Tucker's and Blue Hole would be the better choices.

These operators will point you to the best places to check out via the motor boat, and even give an accompanying map. Expect to pay around $200, plus fuel costs. They may also offer equipment such as snorkeling gear.

Take note of the operators' restrictions regarding areas you may venture to. When you get to your destinations, you might want to set up a picnic site, and enjoy the privacy of a secluded beach.

If you are looking to prepare your own itinerary and you have the money to spare, you may event rent a yacht or a large sail boat. Even if you haven't saved that much, if there is a large group of people who can contribute toward the cost, you might still be able to rent a boat.

Snorkeling

You can still witness Bermuda's magnificent marine life despite lack of training or certification in SCUBA diving. Snorkeling will allow you to do just that. Rentals of snorkeling gear (including snorkel, mask, and fins) usually cost around $20 per day. That's way cheaper compared to buying your own at a shop in Hamilton. After all, the reefs are located near the shore so you don't have to venture too far out. You can just rent a boat and snorkeling gear to set up your own snorkeling trip, or opt for snorkeling spots that are closer to the beach. You can go snorkeling at almost any beach, but many people agree that the best spots are Tobacco Bay and Church bay.

Church Bay is near Fairmont Southampton and is easy to get to because it is part of the main bus route. The beach is a bit rocky, and the water, a little choppy but the reef is pretty close to the shore. Expect to see a lot of large parrotfish and other colorful species.

Tobacco Bay has gentler and shallower waters so even children can enjoy the place. It's also surrounded by limestone formations – perfect for a nature or geology enthusiast. There's a beach bar where you can buy food and drinks, and a concession stand for snorkeling equipment.

Fishing

Sport fishing is popular not just for tourists and locals alike. You may go deep sea fishing if you're adventurous and you have the money to spare. Boat captains will take the boat out to Challenger Bank, which is about 13 miles off the coast of Bermuda, or to Argus Bank, which is about 20 miles. The best months for this are May to October. Potential catch includes Marlin and tuna. Operators typically keep the catch to offset costs, but you may ask to have some.

You can just go reef fishing if you are on a budget. Since the reefs are closer to the shore, the boat doesn't need much fuel. You may hire reef fishing operators for a few hours. Options include Island Tour Centre's reef fishing trips via the Royal navy Dockyard, or Baxter's Reef Fishing. The rates cover tackle rental and bait. Potential catch includes barracuda, chub, and snappers. You can also rent your own small fishing boats; just take note of the operators' restrictions on where you can take the boat.

If you want a more relaxed fishing activity, you can just go sport fishing. It's the most popular among the locals, and you might just make friends with some if you go that route. Some of the best fishing spots include Watford Bridge near Somerset County Squire and Watch Hill Park near John Smith's Bay, and Somerset Long Bay. You'll have to get or rent your own tackle, although most locals just use lines. There are many shops that sell or offer rentals of fishing equipment in the area. You can rent some for a few days. Expect to catch bonefish, pompano and jacks.

Before you venture out to fish, remember that there are rules and regulations in place. There are certain protected species such as parrotfish that must be returned to the sea. There are also bag limits for certain species. All fixed fishing gear such as traps and pots are prohibited. You'll need a license for spearfishing and lobster fishing. Check out sites dedicated to Bermuda fishing rules and regulations for more details.

Golf

You are pretty much spoiled for choice when it comes to golfing in Bermuda. In fact, there was a time when the sheer number of its golf courses (considering its overall land area) is what the island was known for. The Bermuda Golf Academy and Driving Range has a miniature golf course and driving range. Belmont Hills Golf Club is an 18-hole golf course. It's also near a luxury resort and spa. There is also the Port Royal golf course managed by the government. It is located near Hamilton. The Turtle Hill Golf club is a par-3 gold course located in the grounds of a luxurious hotel.

Kayaking

If you are fit and would like to discover "hidden" gems such as coves and secluded beaches, this activity is for you. Kayaking is small and maneuverable, allowing you to truly explore the island(s). It's also silent so you can get up close and personal with Bermuda wildlife and not cause a lot of disruption. Kayaks offered by operators in Bermuda are stable and buoyant and is designed in such a way that makes it easy to get in and get out. It's a safer choice because it drastically reduces the likelihood of getting trapped. There are plenty of operators that offer kayak rentals; these include Blue Hole Water Sports, Dive Bermuda, H2O sports, and the Island Tour Centre, among a slew of other options.

Walking and Trail Hiking

Bermuda, being a subtropical country, has beautiful weather and one of the best ways to take advantage of that is to take a walking tour. If you rent a bicycle, you can save a lot of time getting from one destination to another. Just prepare comfortable clothing – particularly the breathable kind that wicks away sweat (available in most sporting goods store) and walking, running, or trail hiking shoes. You may explore the area in your own if you have a GPS device (like a smartphone) or a map. If you like birdwatching, you absolutely should visit the Spittal Pond Nature Reserve, a 24-hectare sanctuary for resident and migratory fowl. This nature reserve features scenic trails and footpaths.

You may also join a guided Bermuda nature hike where you can explore the Railway Trail and Fort Scaur, an area spanning not just a historical fort but also 22 acres of beautiful parkland, picnic areas, scenic trails and a rocky shoreline. The tour also includes a visit to a 178th century estate, and you get to experience magnificent views and see interesting flora and fauna.

If you happen to be in Bermuda on a Sunday, you're in luck. You may join Bermuda's Walking Club. They meet at 7 am on Sundays to take a 6 to 7 mile walk along awesome scenic routes. It's free and you'll get a chance to hang out with locals and get a peek at the life of the islanders.

If you are a trail hiking enthusiast, you might also want to visit Cooper's Island. This unspoiled nature reserve is located in the southeastern tip of the main island. It features trails you can traverse to your heart's content and breathtaking views of Castle Harbour. Through this area, you can also get to several popular beaches such as Turtle Beach, as well as other beautiful beaches like Annie's Bay and Clearwater Beach. It's perfect if you're looking to build an itinerary for a day and you want to fill it with picnics, bird watching, snorkeling, swimming, and hiking.

It's also a great spot for those who are interested in wildlife. It has been under active restoration since 1995 and the restored salt marsh and pond area has a boardwalk so you can easily explore the place. You might see giant land crabs and birds like kingfishers and herons. There is even a wildlife observation tower. Get there if you want to try spotting whales.

If you like taking the scenic route, you may try exploring the St George parish located at the eastern part of Bermuda. This suggested route is a combination of a little urban exploration mixed with some beach time, nature walks, and exploring unique buildings such as forts. Ideally, the docks at St George will be your starting point. Walk toward the beach at Tobacco Bay from there. You'll see the Unfinished Church along the way, a remarkable Gothic building with quite the history. The ruins are what's left of an unfinished project which was brought by a storm damaging an existing church and parishioners disagreeing about whether to build a new one or to just repair the old church.

Keep on walking until you get to the St George golf course, an 18-hole golf course. Keep on walking until you see Tobacco Bay and just follow the path that leads there. If you got there early in the morning, try snorkeling! You can also just keep on walking until you reach a hill and then a cove called Coot Pond. You can then retrace your steps and this time, instead of going to the bay, choose the other path (Barry Road) until you reach Fort St. Catherine – an impressive fort featuring historical artifacts, exhibits and a moat (albeit a dry one) that can be accessed by a drawbridge!

From there, you can pay an admission fee to get in, or just enjoy the view from the outside. Keep on walking through Barry Road until you get to Alexandra Battery & Beach. From there, you can visit more forts and some restaurants and pubs. Go get or download a map of St George, or any other detailed tourist map of any parish in Bermuda so you can plan your own scenic route walk. You can also visit Google maps for more details.

The Old Town of St. George

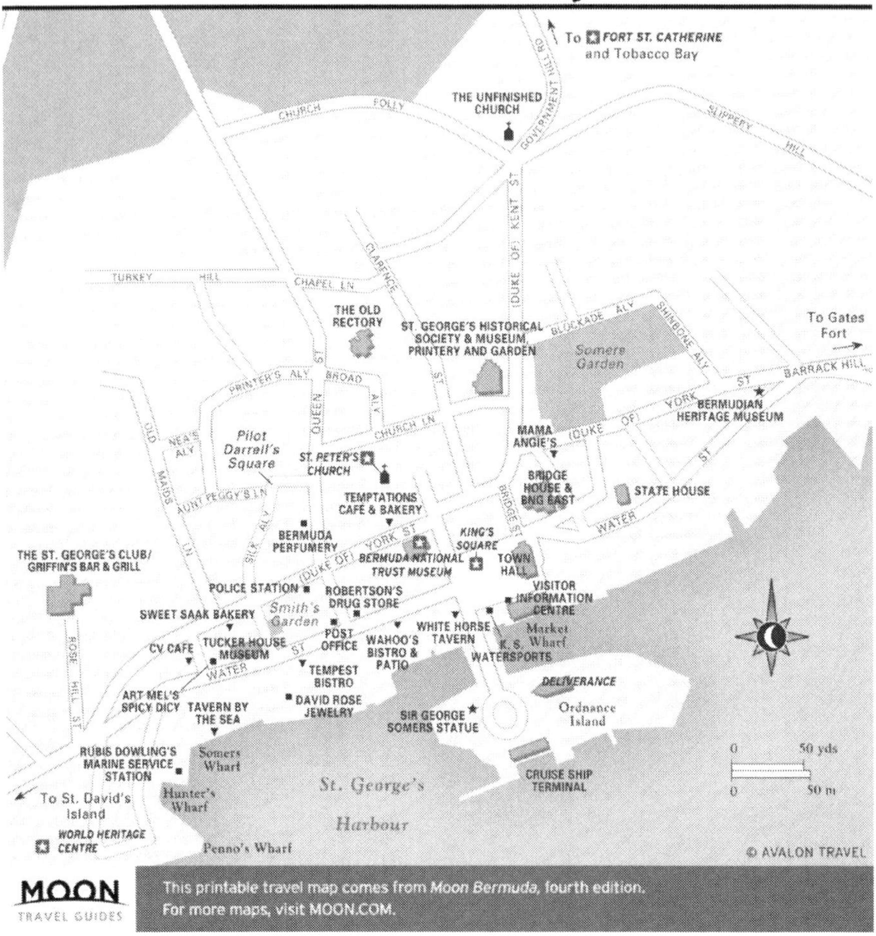

Image source: Moon.com

Other Activities

You may go windsurfing in the area but you really shouldn't bring your own board. You will not be able to get them on any public transportation. It's best to just rent equipment from operators such as Blue Hole Water Sports.

If you want an underwater experience that is a bit similar to scuba diving minus the expenses and training required, you may try helmet diving. You'll get to explore reefs in relatively shallow water wearing specialized equipment that allow you to breathe underwater and keep you from floating to the surface. Hartley's helmet Diving is the only operator for this activity. It's best to do this during the warmest months.

You may also have a round of squash and tennis at some of the hotels in the area.

Chapter 8. Where to Eat

For many people, the best part in any vacation is to that they get to indulge in good – and sometimes unique (bordering on the exotic) food. Bermudian cuisine is pretty extensive, ranging from scrumptious seafood like fish chowder and broiled lobsters to the Oriental like canton noodles. Due to its British roots, tea at 3 o'clock in the afternoon is to be experienced with friends or family.

This section is about the more popular food haunts in the area. There are also drinks that are associated with Bermuda which tourists should absolutely try.

What You Need To Know When Dining In Bermuda

Water is only semi-potable in Bermuda. Many homes and buildings rely on rainfall as a source of available though. If you are sensitive to the quality of drinking water, it is advisable that you order bottled soda pops or bottled water. It is customary in most restaurants to add ice to beverages. The water being used to make the ice might be made from said water.

Almost all of the restaurants in Bermuda automatically add the tips for the waiter on your bill so don't worry about leaving any. The amount is around 15%. It's actually a controversial issue these days but it can't be helped. There are, however, some restaurants that do not engage in such practice – Mad Hatters, Swizzle Inn and Specialty Inn.

Mid-Range Restaurants

The Bermuda restaurants featured in this travel guide has a wide range of offerings that have received rave reviews, such as Pan-Fried Chicken and Lamb Kebabs with Yogurt and Mint. Here are mid-range restaurants in the city of Hamilton and nearby areas. Included are the address, phone number, type of cuisine and the website for your reference. Have fun in your gastronomic adventure!

The Hog Penny

Address: 5 Burnaby St, Hamilton HM 12, Bermuda
Phone Number: +1 (441) 292-2534
Website: hogpennypub
Store Hours: open for lunch until dinner, Mon-Sat (11:30 until 1AM)
Cuisine: Oriental, Mediterranean, American

What can $30 give you in Bermuda? You can spend it in a snazzy bar and order appetizers or hop on to Hog Penny and fill your tummy with three mouthwatering meals! Here at the Hog Penny you can taste Thai favorites like chicken satay; Persian picks like Lamb Moussaka or Oriental crusted tuna with sesame and canton noodles. How about a $50 3-course meal? Still, this restaurant will give you some of the best of Bermuda at an affordable price.

For appetizers, try the mouthwatering Carpaccio de salmon. It is served with hollandaise sauce, vegetable salsa and fruits. For entrees, have the tomato roast pasta and salmon, wahoo or hog fish in truffle oil and parmesan.

Do not leave Hog Penny without tasting their tiramisu or choklit brownies. Did we mention the snapper topped with lobster crust toppings and asparagus, pumpkin mash potatoes?

Mad Hatters Restaurant

Address: 22 Richmond Road, Hamilton, HM 08, Bermuda
Phone Number: +1 (441) 297-6231
Website: madhatters
Store Hours: open for lunch until dinner, Mon-Sat (12 until 9PM)
Cuisine: Thai, North-American, European

Care for some swordfish with mango salsa and a salad with walnuts and apples in honey Dijon dressing for lunch? Dine with who's who in town for dinner and be served with salmon that is grilled to perfection. It also comes with delicious crab cakes in ginger and sweet chili.

Don't forget to cap the night with a glass of red wine for only $34. All meals are single-serve but will make you feel one with the "stars" of Bermuda. Service charge is not reflected in the bill. However, this restaurant appreciates gratuity or tip based on the quality of food and service received.

Art Mels Spicy Dicy

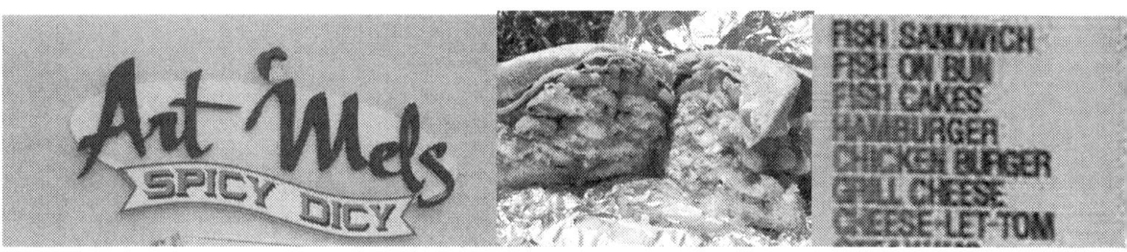

Address: 22 Richmond Road, Hamilton, HM 08, Bermuda
Phone Number: +1 (441) 295-3965
Website: artmels
Store Hours: open for lunch until dinner, Mon-Sat (12 until 8:30PM)
Cuisine: Contemporary, American, Bermudian

Fried fish sandwiches, salad and soups, Art Mels Spicy Dicy can offer one of the most affordable meals in this side of town. Located in St. George and Hamilton, the eatery attracts tourists who fly to Bermuda on a strict diet. The meals are liberally served on big plates but small on the tab plate for sure. Go home with a $20 tab for a 3-course meal for lunch or dinner.

Wok Express Restaurant

Address: 180 Middle Road, Southampton SN 03
Phone Number: +1 (441) 238-8888
Website: wokexpress
Store Hours: open for lunch until dinner, Mon-Sun (11:30 until 10PM)
Cuisine: Oriental, Italian, Mediterranean, American

Come to Wok Express and get Japanese and Chinese food under one roof. Where else can you savor the different tempura - shrimp, tuna or crab and not to mention their maki. In case you got tired of eating oriental cuisine and would like to play it safe, go Italian with fried Calamari, chicken Wings, Caesar salad, Panini with fish, chicken or turkey fills. Their menu goes on and on with a touch of Persian dishes like shawarma.
If you still can't make up your mind, they have fish and chips to fill your growling tummy. The dishes are affordably priced below $20.

House of India

Address: Park View Plaza, 58A North St., City of Hamilton, Bermuda, HM 17
Phone Number: +1 (441) 295-6450
Website: houseofindia
Store Hours: open for lunch until dinner, Mon-Fri (11:30 until 9:45PM)
Cuisine: Indian

If you happen to end up tight on a budget, there is a restaurant that serves food that costs really expensive. Order food at the House of India and go back to your hotel feeling satisfied.

They serve meals that cost $11 to $15. This is not bad at all if you happen to get hungry during your day trips to the beach. Their restaurant had been in business since 1955 and has deliciously served spicy food for their clientele. Did you know that they offer the chicken chetinad? This dish is extremely spicy but you can always request for a non-spicier dish like the Tandoori Chicken. Namaste!

Somerset Country Squire Pub & Restaurant

8 York Street, Lower South East Building, St. George's, GE05
Phone Number: +1 (441) 297-0208
Cuisine: Bermudian, Contemporary
Store Hours: open daily from 10AM until 5:30PM (during the winter season, lunch is limited to a couple of days), bar open until late.

This is a fine restaurant in Hamilton City where you can have a meal at $15. Majority of the guests have appreciated the warm and true nature of Bermudian hosts. Grab a bite to eat at the restaurant and order Bermuda's classic fish chowder until your main course of Lobster in garlic sauce arrives. The most expensive meal in this place costs $50 and it is the crab legs that are too difficult to catch during high tide.

As a tourist, you are often told not to stay outdoors at nightfall. If you happen to take a late dinner, chances are, the waiters from this restaurant will call a cab for you to make sure you arrive at your destination in one piece. Being friendly to strangers is one of the character traits of Bermudian residents.

Bonefish Bar & Grill

Address: Royal Naval Dockyard, 6 Dockyard Terrace, Sandys MA01, Bermuda
Phone Number: +1 (441) 234-5151
Website: bonefishbermuda
Cuisine: Mediterranean
Store Hours: open daily from 11:30AM until 5 PM, bar opens from 6PM until 3AM

Savour the best food in Bermuda at an affordable price. At Bonefish Bar & Grill, order their mahi mahi, sea bass or yellow fin tuna and you'd never go wrong. This restaurant may look expensive from the outside but is rated as one of the affordably priced places to visit in Bermuda.

Smokin' Barrel Bermuda

Address: 1 Water Front Park, Front Street, Hamilton, Bermuda
Phone Number: +1 (441) 537-6653
Website: smokinbarrelbermuda
Cuisine: Caribbean, Bermudian
Store Hours: open daily from 10AM to 8:30PM

Have you ever ordered food from mobile trucks before? In the US there are several Mexican restaurants that follow the set-up. Here in Bermuda, you may have the chance to taste the fine flavors of the Caribbean through the Smokin' Barrel. All the dishes in the menu are guaranteed to taste so good but easy on the wallet. All meals have an average price of $20 and goes real low at $8. Enjoy a huge serving of Pulled Pork BBQ cornbread sandwich for $12; partner it will quinoa kale salad for $10.

DeGraff's Lunch Counter

Address: North corner, City Hall Parking lot, Bermuda
Phone Number: +1 (441) 799-3904
Cuisine: Traditional Bermudian
Store Hours: open daily from 10AM to 8:30PM

Now that mobile trucks are slowly making its way to Bermuda, a few tourists may hae bumped on one. There is actually a lunch counter at the parking lot of Hamilton's City Hall that may be been in business since 1939. Yes, it is that old already but if you ask the locals, they know the look of this truck for ages. Order their special Bermudian beef pie or the mouthwatering burgers. They also serve fish cakes, fish fillets, and steak for about $9.

Winky Dinky Dog

Address: Woodlands Rd, Hamilton, Bermuda
Phone Number: +1 (441) 535-1648
Cuisine: Traditional Bermudian
Store Hours: open daily from 10AM to 3PM (subject to close due to high winds)

For as low as $5, you can grab juicy 6-inch beef frankfurters with coleslaw, juice and chips. They change their hotdog for the day and spread it out throughout the week. This is an exciting chance for you to taste a variety of hotdogs. It's best to drop by from 10AM until 3PM.

Bermuda's Cest La Vie Dining

If you saved enough for your Bermudian trip, try dining in the following upscale restaurants.

Lobster Pot

Address: 6 Bermudiana Road, City of Hamilton
Phone Number: +1 (441) 292-6898
Website: lobsterpot
Store Hours: open for lunch until dinner, Mon-Fri (11:30 until 5:30PM)
Cuisine: Southern American, Contemporary, Bermudian

Are you craving for succulent pan seared tuna, steamed lobsters, snapper that is herb crusted & baked or Bermuda's traditional salted cod fish cakes? Lobster Pot is here to serve you these! They are priced at $35 a meal. Indulge in these one of a kind fresh catch ingredients that when cooked are indeed mouthwatering and unforgettable. Lobster Pot is up in ranks of posh, pricey and sassy restaurants but while you are in Bermuda, you must not let this opportunity pass you by.

Bistro J

Address: Chancery Lane, Hamilton HM 12, Bermuda
Phone Number: +1 (441) 296-8546
Website: portocall
Store Hours: open at lunch until 10PM, Mon-Sat
Cuisine: Oriental, Italian, Mediterranean and Bermudian

Are you ready for a finer taste of Bermuda? Go and have an appetizer of grilled scallops in avocado relish and some tortilla rounds. For your main course, why not try Bistro J's rendition of Mahi Mahi with chili and honey glaze. It is served over healthy basmati rice. Average price is around $25. The servings can be shared by two people.

Blu Bar & Grill

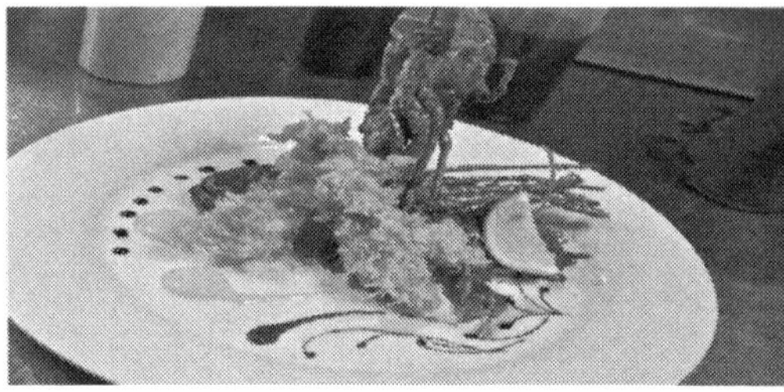

Address: 25 Belmont Hills Drive, Warwick, Bermuda
Phone Number: +1 (441) 232-2323
Website: blu
Store Hours: open for dinner Mon-Sun 6 - 9pm
Cuisine: American, European, Oriental

The catch for the day is what you will have for dinner! Imagine ordering broiled Bermuda lobsters cooked in mustard and cognac. All the food you have dreamt of is yours for just $25! What if there are smoked salmons with sour cream. Will you stay in Bermuda for a little bit longer?

Barracuda Grill Restaurant

Address: 5 Burnaby Hill, Hamilton HM10, Bermuda
Phone Number: +1 (441) 292-1609
Website: barracudagrill
Store Hours: open for lunch until dinner, Mon-Fri, 12-10PM, Bar until 11:30PM
Cuisine: Contemporary, Bermudian

Want to indulge in modern cuisine and good steaks and seafood? This is the place to be! Try the fried calamari at Barracuda Grill with blue cheese dip and you will want for more. They also have the fish chowder as well as kale and squash salad. For dinner, why don't you order their best-seller dish seared hogfish that come with coconut bamboo rice and shitake mushrooms! All these wonderful dishes are priced at $30 on an average.

Devils Isle Restaurant

Address: 19 Burnaby Hill, Hamilton HM11, Bermuda
Phone Number: +1 (441) 292-3284
Website: devilsisle
Store Hours: open for breakfast until dinner, 8-5PM, Mon-Sat
Cuisine: Contemporary, International, European

Bermudians are known for their healthy lifestyle and this particular restaurant offers exactly the same rich goodness. All their ingredients are organic, flavorful and satisfying to the tummy. For breakfast, why not try their quinoa, eggs and kale? For lunch, they serve unbelievably tasty Scottish salmon with fermented green tea gremolata with asparagus and roasted veggies. Dinner time will be unforgettable with their chargrilled octopus with aioli dip and roasted vegetables. All dishes are within the range of $30 but the servings can be shared by 2 people.

Bella Vista Bar and Grill

Address: Port Royal Golf Course, 5 Port Royal Drive, Southampton SB03, Bermuda
Phone Number: +1 (441) 232-0100
Website: bellavistagrill
Store Hours: open for breakfast until dinner, 11:30AM-10:30OM, Mon-Sat
Cuisine: Italian, International

Eat the familiar Italian cuisine with a Bermudian twist. Who can go wrong with the classic Pepperoni pizza for $24? Wait till dinner comes and you get to taste the scallops and chorizo over risotto for $40! Large servings are great for 2 to 3 people.

Four Ways Inn

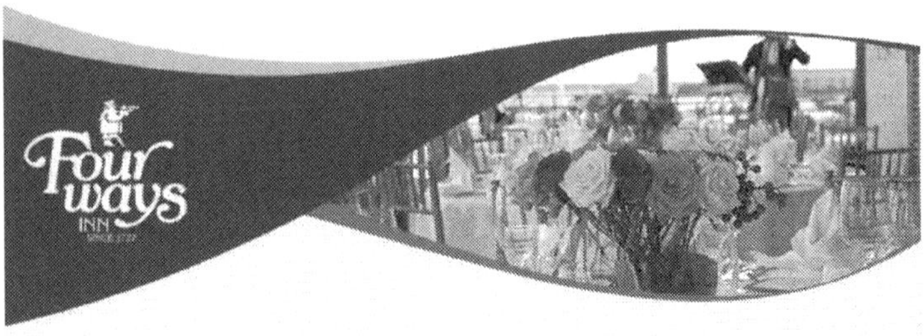

Address: 1 Middle Road, Paget PG 01, Bermuda
Phone Number: +1 (441) 236-6517
Website: fourwaysinn
Store Hours: Monday to Saturday
Cuisine: European, American, Mediterranean

This restaurant is known as one of the most upscale restaurants, serving expensive meals. Have you ever tried sautéed mussels and later on grilled to perfection? This is your chance to sink your teeth on their escargot in cream sauce with Caesar salad for $25.

It's just the beginning of a scrumptious buffet so order some of the famous appetizers at Four Ways Inn – the Foie Gras in Fig essence for $30. If the chef woke up on the right side of the bed, he may just prepare his best-seller as your main course. His 8 ounce Filet Mignon and Scampi! You need to hold in your breath since it is a $50 meal! For the entirety of your lunch or dinner, you will go home with a whopping $105 tab.

Port O' Call

Address: 87 Front Street, City of Hamilton, Bermuda
Phone Number: + 1 (441) 295 5373
Website: portocall
Store Hours: Open daily from 12PM to 10PM (Happy Hour at the bar 4PM to 7PM)
Cuisine: American, Italian

When you are staying in the posh side of Bermuda, one of the best places to have dinner is at the Port O' Call. Enjoy the crisp air by the beach by Al fresco or get intimate in their air conditioned halls. No other restaurant has received good praises for their mouthwatering menu.

Dinner is their favorite meal of the day since the chef over at Port O' Call has prepared an $85 meal. Imagine the succulent 44 ounce Porter House steak paired with Truffle fries. Enjoy a glass or even consume a bottle of the finest wines to cap the delicious buffet. Their desserts come with a touch of Italian for you to enjoy.

La Trattoria Restaurant

Address: 23 Washington Lane, Hamilton HM 11, Bermuda
Phone Number: + 1 (441) 295-1877
Website: latrattoria
Store Hours: Open daily from 11:30AM to 10PM
Cuisine: Italian

Bermuda is indeed rich in history and it reflects in its restaurants as well. This Italian restaurant opened its doors in 1979 and since then provides the best meals and desserts. It is of common knowledge that dining in Bermuda is expensive; wait until you taste its scrumptious dishes! A $30 meal is not enough for one person since the flavor is good; you have no choice to order for more. For a 4-course meal, you will have close to $100 to your tab. Italian food is known for huge servings for they are known to share food with the family. Here is a tip: their best seller is their pizza. Do not leave town without ordering one! Of course pizza slices do come in large proportions. Try to eat it the Italian way by folding two sides together. Otherwise you need to pay an additional $2 to let waiters cut the slices into smaller sizes.

Victoria Grill

Address: 29 Victoria Street, Hamilton City, Bermuda
Phone Number: + 1 (441) 296-5050
Website: victoriagrill
Store Hours: Open from Mon-Sat from 12:30PM to 10PM
Cuisine: Southern Coastal (truly Bermudian with a twist)

Since Bermuda is known for their aristocratic taste in food, where else can you order a simple macaroni and cheese with truffle? They have this remarkable entrée for a whopping $30 per plate. It is customary of course to order the Bermudian seafood and this is your chance to taste a sophisticated shrimp! Victoria Grill calls their scampi as crevette cocktail and these shrimps are the jumbo ones. This appetizer will cost you around $16.

Tips On Dining Out As A Tourist

Search for restaurants that have a long line of customers. There are times when you do not know where to eat. Just look at restaurants with long queues since it is a proof that they serve good food there. It is also good to search for diners and off-the-road food establishments to experience the authentic cuisine that country is famous to serve.

Ask the waiter for his restaurant's best sellers so you are not likely to go wrong.

Research about a destination's off season. The worst part in your trip is to look forward to a particular kind of food only to find out that restaurateurs have closed their shops for the holidays.

Research about a destination's peak season. Waiting for a table during festivals and public holidays often turns off tourists. The advantage over the long wait is that there is free food for everyone's consumption.

You need to acquaint yourself with the destination's cuisine when you visit it for the first time. Try not to look for US fast food chains such as the Golden Archers. They are, sad to say, absent in Bermuda. Even though the Colonel is finger-lickin' present on the island, a combo meal can cost you about $11. As the saying goes, when in Bermuda, eat what the Bermudians eat!

Chapter 9. Bermudian Nightlife

Daytime is for dining, shopping, lounging, and water activities. Enjoy Bermuda at sunset and it will definitely look different. Here are several bars you can visit and add to your travel blog when you get home. Keep in mind that some bars require standard attire, but some require some dressing up. Go ahead and dress up to the nines!

Hamilton is your best bet if you want to relax and unwind at nightclubs and bars. The interesting pubs truly reminiscent of English culture are not just the reason that tourists enjoy Bermuda nightlife. Unlike some tourist destinations, Bermuda nightlife atmosphere can change by the season.

You see, during summer, the after-dark discos are mostly hot and in. During winter, there is no other choice but get drunk inside pubs. However, almost all Bermuda's hotels have in-house nightlife action. Here you can sing along with bar hosts, dance with their dance instructors or even enjoy a night of stand-up comedy entertainment.

Flanagan's Irish Pub & Restaurant

Address: Emporium Building, 69 Front Street, Hamilton (Pembroke Parish)
Phone Number: +1 (441) 295-8299
Website: flanagans
Bar Hours: Mon-Sun until 1AM (Happy Hour is from 4-7PM every Fridays)
Attire: Upper Casual

Drinks:

Draft beer and bottled beer - $9.50/glass, $28/pitcher
Ciders - $14/glass, $40/pitcher
Cocktails - $11 (Island concoctions) $13 Martinis

Flanagans serves draft beers from the UK, Denmark, Ireland, Holland, USA and Belgium.

Margarita's Grill

Address: 12 Bermudiana Road, Hamilton
Phone Number: +1 (441) 296-3330
Website: margaritas
Bar Hours: Mon-Sat from 5PM until 2AM

Attire: Upper Casual

Drinks:
Margaritas, mojitos, cocktails and martinis - $9.75/glass, $40/pitcher

Every Wednesdays, you can dance the night away at their salsa and bachata night. There is no cover charge to worry about. Everything you order is what you pay. There are also tapas, burgers and other meals that can be ordered before and during your stay at the Bermudian hotspot. This isn't a dining spot though so don't expect the food to blow your mind.

Club Aqua

Address: 1 Snorkel Park Beach, Royal Naval Dockyard
Phone Number: +1 (441) 234-3100
Bar Hours: Mon-Wed-Thurs-Sat from 10PM until 3AM ($10 cover charge)
Attire: Upper Casual

Drinks: Hard, bottled beer, draft bear, cocktails, non-alcoholic beverages start from $10 to $40. Drinks may be ordered in glasses or pitchers.

Enjoy the Bermudian night al-fresco at Club Aqua. No other bar is designed in such a way that guests can easily watch the ships docked at the Royal Naval Dockyard. Drinks and munchies are affordable and delicious.

Light Nightclub (White Horse Pub & Restaurant)

Address: 8 Kings Square, St. George's GE 05 Bermuda
Phone Number: +1 (441) 297-1838
Bar Hours: Mon-Fri from 5PM until 7PM
Website: whitehorsebermuda
Attire: Upper Casual

Drinks: Happy Hour $5 on regular drinks and beer.

Light Nightclub is believed to be the #1 bar and nightclub in St. George. They restaurant opened to the public since 1930 but it was only in 2010 became the primary stop of Bermudian locals and tourists who plan to have a party night with friends. What sets this club apart from the others is their lights and sounds display that bounces off the walls of the pub. Live spinning from resident disc jockeys makes this place a rocking sensation until the wee hours of the morning.

The Pickled Onion

Address: 53 Front Street, Hamilton
Phone Number: +1 (441) 295-2263

Bar Hours: Mon-Fri from 11AM until 1AM
Website: thepickledonion
Attire: Upper Casual

Drinks: Cocktails are served at $10.25 per glass. Wines vary in price depending on the make and year. Price usually ranges from as low as $28 to as intoxicating as a $250 bottle of Dom Perignon.

Rocking the Hamilton side of Bermuda is The Pickled Onion. This amazing bar has been operating since 1998. The most-sought after pale is called the Dark and Stormy. This beverage has attracted both local and tourists to make the pub one of their first stops after sunset.

Frog & Onion Pub Bermuda

Address: The Cooperage, Royal Naval Dockyard, Sandy's Parish
Phone Number: +1 (441) 234-2900
Bar Hours: open daily from 11:30am to midnight

Drinks: Handcrafted beers are sold for $8.95. They are the different kinds of ale and lager served in a pint glass. If you want to taste different kinds of Bermudian beer, they offer small servings amounting to $13.95. Cocktails are sold for $10.25 per glass while their wines range from $10.25 to as much as $80.

Chapter 10. Tours around Bermuda Island

There is more to Bermuda than delicious food and the beach. Make your stay in the island an unforgettable one by joining different activities. The first step is to tour this tranquil and enchanting island in more ways than one. There are the dive spots where you can experience the turquoise waters and experience how it is to swim near the tropical coral reefs. We already touched upon the activities you may try in a previous chapter but if you'd rather not explore the island on your own and you'd appreciate assistance from tour operators, here are some options.

Water Tours

Bermuda is known for its crystal clear waters and remarkable marine life and history. Take these following destinations and see for yourself. Don't forget to bring along your camera for take snapshots of your precious moments.

Destiny Waters Glass-Bottom Tour

Book with: Destiny Water Tours Bermuda
Phone Number: +1 (441) 292-7103
Website: destinywatertours

Take a glass-bottom view of amazing shipwrecks, corals and marine life aboard the M.V. Destiny. Take a boat ride and be awed with the interesting design of the boat that will make your underwater viewing much easier. The waters are too deep and if you are not prepared to go snorkeling just yet, you may opt to sail on a yacht with Captain Cookie Brown. Enjoy the glass boat tour for $35/head. If you are travelling with a large group, the boat is also available at a charter rate at $650/hour (minimum 2 hours trip). The tour usually begins at 10AM and leaves the dock of the Grotto Bay Beach Resort. The yacht can accommodate as much as 100 passengers.

Crystal Caves & Fantasy Caves

Address: 8 Crystal Caves Road, off Wilkinson Avenue Bay, Hamilton Parish, Bermuda
Phone Number: +1 (441) 293-0640
Website: caves

Tour the island and witness different cave formations that run through the Cahow Lake. The cave is 120 feet deep that can be seen within 30 minutes. The only catch in this tour is how to get up since going down the steep stairs is easier to begin with. This cave is safe since it is a guided tour that will cost you $22. If you plan to bring along children, those under 5 years old can come in for free. Children 5 years old and above can join the guided tour for only $12.

Powerboat Round-the-Island Tour

Dock: Royal Naval Dockyard, Bermuda
Address: Ireland Island North, Bermuda
Phone Number: +1 (441) 236-1300
Website: islandtourscentre

At precisely 1000 hours, join a high-speed adventure around the island for only $110. Your captain awaits you at the WildCat as he slices through the Bermudian crystal blue waters to bring your to Horseshoe Bay, Tucker Town and St. George's. For three hours and 30 minutes, this narrated tour will bring you to Bermuda's past and guide you to the present. Keep in mind that you should be at least twenty minutes earlier than the departure time. Of course, any trip is worth the wait when the time to eat comes along! This tour will take you to one of the trendy restaurants in St. George's for a filling snack (exclusive of tour fee).

Bermuda Reef Explorer

Dock: Royal Naval Dockyard, Bermuda
Address: Suite 251, 48 Par-la-Ville Road, Hamilton HM 11, Bermuda
Phone Number: +1 (441) 535-7333
Website: bermudareefexplorer

The reef explorer is one huge boat ride that will take you to the most exciting places on sea. Glass-bottom boats are a hit in the island since you can view under the sea without getting wet! There are times when the reef explorer detaches their flooring so you can have a chance to dive in to the crystal blues. This is their safe move to make sure that no stingrays are within your vicinity. Your choices are few but each tour kind is definitely worth your time! Should you should the Reef Explorer's Pirate Adventure, it costs around $45 for adults and $20 for kids. They also have a complimentary ticket for kids under the age of six. Adults are on the edge of their seats since for their guided tour fee, a complimentary rum swizzle is included.

Hartley's Undersea (Helmet) Walk

Dock: Royal Naval Dockyard, Bermuda
Address: Suite 251, 48 Par-la-Ville Road, Hamilton HM 11, Bermuda
Phone Number: +1 (441) 234-3535
Website: hartleybermuda

You might not want to Bermuda without having the chance to walk under the sea! Here at Hartley's undersea walk, participants get to wear helmets in order to breathe under water. It is not like snorkeling where you got to hold your breath for a few seconds and dip your mask to see the nearby marine life. The "helmet walk" costs around $95/diver. Get to be one with the sea creatures for thirty to forty minutes. However, the length of the entire trip may take three or four hours.

Be at the Heritage Warf twenty minutes before 9AM. Diving is included in this tour where the waters are from eight to twelve feet deep. Make sure that you know how to swim before engaging in this activity. For your peace of mind, authorities in Bermuda value your safety. Make sure to fill up the insurance form before sailing to sea.

When you have decided to walk under the sea, keep in mind that the water temperatures vary per month. Make sure that you log on to Bermuda's weather website. April waters have a chilly 66 to 68 degree temperature. By August to October, it will be a warm 84 degrees and gets colder at 70 degrees by December.

If you are wondering what fish will you see during your sea tour, Hartley's have recently reported the following species: angelfish, hogfish, dory, red speckled hind, squirrelfish, snappers, lizard fish, goldentailed moray eel and trumpet fish! Once you spot them, it is advisable to carry your waterproof camera so you can take pictures to show your family.

Walking Tours

Rediscover the rich history of Bermuda by visiting museums near your hotel. If you are checked in near the Royal Naval Dockyard, head on to the National Museum of Bermuda. Here, almost 30,000 exhibits are showcased on the history of the island as well as the development of its culture.

Bermuda National Museum

Dock: Royal Naval Dockyard Complex
Address: The Keep, Maritime Ln, MA 01, Bermuda
Phone Number: +1 (441) 234-1418
Website: bermudanationalmuseum

Your tour includes different houses that were built in the early 1800s. The government of Bermuda has successfully restored the place to make it look as if you have stepped inside a time machine. Take the Commissioner's House as an example. Tourists will have the chance to witness the oldest cast iron house. This Gregorian architectural fortress houses rare coins used during the Slavery Period.

You can also visit the Shifting House within the walls of The Keep. This is where age-old ammunitions were stored as well as the exact place where Admiral Sir George Somers got shipwrecked in the early 1900s. And speaking of shipwrecks, did you know that a hundred year old yacht that goes by the name of The Dainty can be seen here? When you want to check out the other areas in the island, it is advisable to book a tour in advance for you to maximize your time. Admission costs $15 for adults and comes for free for children below 16 years old. The museum is open from Monday until Sunday, 9:30AM until 5PM.

Bermuda Railway Trail

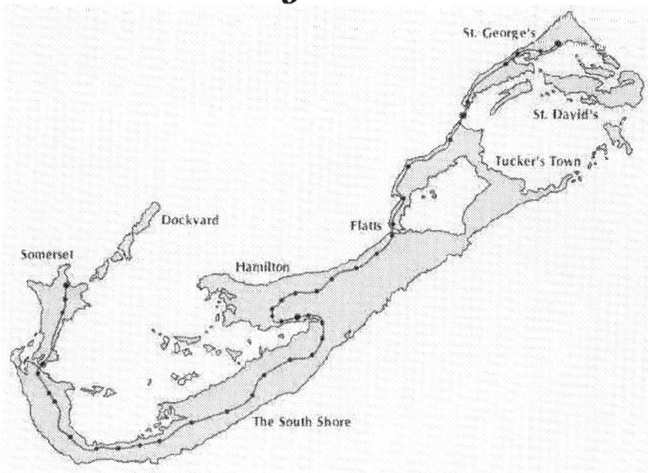

Photo Credit: bermudaonline

For maps: Visitors Service Bureau
Address: Royal Naval Dockyard, 10 Dockyard Terrace, Sandy's Parish
Phone Number: +1 (441) 234 - 3824
Website: bermudarailway

The railway trail is one of Bermuda's oldest tourist destinations where you can reach by bicycle, horseback or foot. Affectionately called "Rattle and Shake," the railway is a place where an old train system once posed as the transportation in Bermuda from 1931 to 1948. Trade bloomed along the railway system since Bermudians used this mode of transportation to load their products to and from the island.

This railway happens to be inaccessible to other forms of transportation. Roughly a 21 mile hike, it is advisable for you to refer to the railway guide provided by the Department of Tourism. Majority of the tourists that traverse alone often find themselves lost and hungry. According to history, the railways closed in 1984 but opened for visitations. The railway trail is free for all visitors. Tourists that plan to hike along the railway path are advised to do it in the morning. Lamp posts are limited in some areas. It is also recommended that you bring along water jugs to keep you hydrated during your tour especially when you are traveling during the day. The sun gets pretty intense around this area.

Paget Marsh With Waterville Gardens Tour

For maps: Visitors Service Bureau

Address: Lovers Lane (off South Road) in the Paget Parish

Contact Bermuda National Trust at Waterville at +1 (441) 236 – 6483 during Tuesday afternoons to reserve a tour.

Admission: Free (you may also explore the marsh on your own)

Operating Hours: From dawn until dusk, daily

How to get there: Get on any bus on routes 2, 7, and 8. Just get off a South Road, and then enter Lovers Lane. Walk a few yards and you'll see a sign board indicating an entrance to Paget Marsh to your left.

Website: http://www.bnt.bm/

You don't have to pay anything to access the peat marsh, but you may want to avail yourself of a handy guided tour. This tour is conducted by BNT (Bermuda National Trust)

While the admission to the Paget Marsh is free, you can avail an excellent guided tour. It is conducted by Bermuda National Trust from Waterville. Guide Tim Rogers first takes you through the gardens at Waterville, where you learn about the unusual plants and features of the traditional garden.

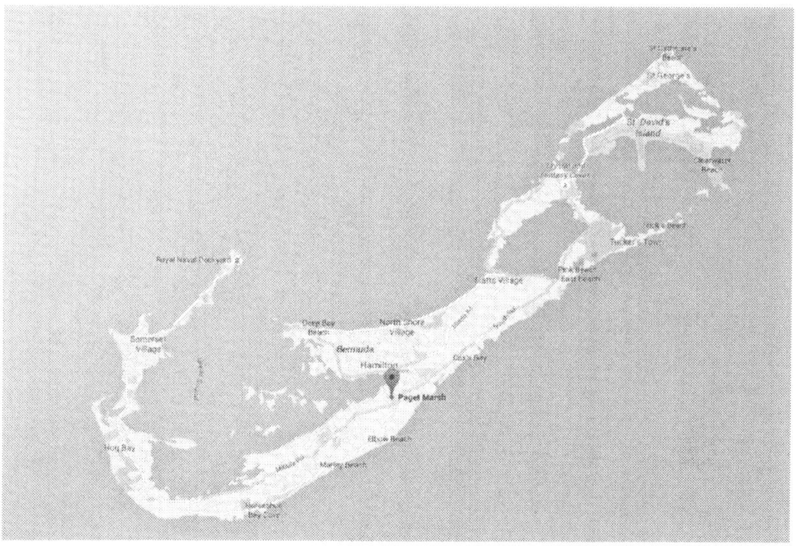

Source: Google Maps

This guided walking tour starts with the Waterville gardens, where you will be introduced to unusual plants and features of this uniquely traditional garden. The two-hour tour also covers a trip to the Paget Marsh, a nature reserve that takes you back to pre-colonial times with original green thriving in its 25 acres. Due to conservation and restoration efforts, the area has remained pretty much unchanged despite all the years that have passed. Visiting Paget Marsh will allow you to take a look at how the Bermuda valleys may have looked like before the first settlers came in and started clearing operations.

The mangroves and forests that are home to palmetto and cedar trees make this a haven for nature lovers. There are so many palmettos that you would see the ground covered by fallen leaf fronds. It’s easier to traverse these days, thanks to a 400-feet boardwalk. Paget Marsh is also home to a diverse range of flora and fauna, including migratory birds.

Chapter 11. Shopping in Bermuda

Here in Bermuda, there are numerous places where you can visit in order to buy souvenirs from your trip. In Bermuda, tourism is their bread and butter. This means that prices are high but you might be able to find bargains.

Specialty Shops

Bluck's (Crystal, China & Porcelain)

Address: 4 West Front Street, City of Hamilton, Pembroke Parish (Central)

Phone Number: +1 (441) 295 – 5367

Website: blucksbermuda

If you are a collector of china, crystals and porcelain, or a loved one is, head on to Bluck's in Pembroke Parish. They are one of the oldest shops in Bermuda that makes sure every product is made to perfection. Who can attest to over 160 years of service of the Bermudian community? The shop offers hand painted porcelain made by different local and foreign companies. The price of a plate ranges from as "low" as $95 to as expensive as $265.

France is known for glass making. Find the most exquisite vases and glasses you can bring back home. Do not worry that it will break en route. Their boxes are made from the most durable and safe materials that will not endanger the expensive wares. The crystal's price ranges from $18 to $175 per piece.

Chatham House

Address: 65 Front Street, City of Hamilton, Pembroke Parish (Central)

Phone Number: +1 (441) 292 - 8422

Website: chathamcigars

Bermudians take credit from the British for their love of cigars. In Bermuda, there is a famous shop that sells the finest as well as expensive cigars. There are different brands to choose from but in choosing out the fine cigars, all you have to do is take a whiff to know that you are buying a $310 cigar from Bolivar or a $400 Montecristo cigar.

Hornburg Calypso Ltd

Address: 45 Front Street, Hamilton, HMFX Bermuda

Phone Number: +1 (441) 295 – 2112

Website: calypsobermuda

This shop caters to every girl's beck and call. At Calypso, several posh brands in the US are making waves in the island. Imagine bags from LongChamp, and swimwear from Ralph Lauren. These brands usually are available back home. Outlets will take care of you in purchasing off-season products. However, here in Bermuda, the top of the line brands have products to test.

Bermuda Beauty and Beyond

Traveling to a place where sun and sand is at the forefront, one must always remember to look gorgeous. When in Bermuda, there are fabulous cosmetic shops to visit. A fine dinner in one of the posh restaurants would cater to smart casual looks. When you run out of makeup or even suntan lotions for your trip to the beach, here are the fancy boutiques in the island to go to.

Phoenix Stores, Ltd.

Address: 3 Reid Street, Hamilton HM 11, Bermuda
Phone Number: +1 (441) 279-5451
Website: phoenixstores

Bermuda's own line up of cosmetics, more and more tourists flock to this boutique to purchase their sun protection and medications. This store happens to be one of the largest shops in Bermuda. It has been in the island since 1902. It specializes in pharmaceutical products and carries different global cosmetic brands. Should you need beauty aids, this is the shop to go to. It initially carried emergency medications to soothe your sun-kissed skin after spending hours on the beach of the Bermuda. The Phoenix Stores is actually a huge one-stop shop where you can also buy your snacks, postcards, and even mobile phone cards! It is open daily from Monday to Saturday.

Alexandra Mosher Studio Jewellery

Address: 7 Reid Street, Lower Level Washington Mall, City of Hamilton, Bermuda
Phone Number: +1 (441) 236 – 9009
Website: alexandramosher

When you fancy fine accessories for a night to remember in Bermuda, why not go to Alexandra Mosher Studio? This jewelry shop has several designs that can cater to your fashion whims. From earrings, necklaces to head loops, the Alexandra Mosher has never-ending choices to tickle your fancy. Open every day from 10AM until 5PM, they are reasonably priced from $95 to $400 per piece; so head on at the shop right now! Did you know that majority of their collections were inspired by the pink beaches of Bermuda? In fact they have named one of their collections as the "Pink Bermuda Sand".

Brown & Co.

Brown & Co.

Address: 35 Front Street, City of Hamilton, Bermuda
Phone Number: +1 (441) 279 – 5443
Website: brownbm

Your Bermuda trip requires that you always hydrate your skin. Head on to the Brown & Co where different multinational brands you have loved in the US are currently making waves in Bermuda! The Body Shop is of course a British brand and since you are in one of Great Britain's offshore territories, it makes its presence felt by many. Brown & Co. also carries an expansive line up of products that cater to nostalgia. They have souvenirs, postcards, books and ladies apparel.

Conclusion

Thank you again for downloading this book!

It was splendid to have written this traveler's guide for you. Do take time document all your Bermuda experiences in your online journal so that others too can learn from you. It is not difficult to visit foreign countries if you know the destination's rules and regulations, and if you are aware of the best spots to visit, and things you absolutely have to try.

Hope you enjoyed the selection of restaurants and beaches to visit in Bermuda. They can all be reached by bus or the taxi. Just get in touch with your hotel's concierge for assistance.

If you enjoyed this book, please take the time to share your thoughts and post a review on Amazon. It'd be greatly appreciated!

Thank you and good luck!

PS: Can I Ask You A Quick Favor?

If you liked the book, please leave a nice review on Amazon! I´d absolutely love to hear your feedback. Every time I read your reviews… you make me smile. I´d be immensely thankful if you go to Amazon now and write down a quick line sharing with me your experience. I personally read ALL the reviews there, and I´m thrilled to hear your feedback and honest motivation. It´s what keeps me going, and helps me improve everyday =)

Please go Amazon Now and Drop A quick review sharing your experience !

***

THANKS!

***

Check Out My Other Books

Below you'll find some of my other popular books that are popular on Amazon and Kindle as well. Simply click on the links below to check them out. Alternatively, you can visit **my author page on Amazon** to see other work done by me.

If the links do not work, for whatever reason, you can simply search for these titles on the Amazon website to find them.

19278409R00075

Printed in Poland
by Amazon Fulfillment
Poland Sp. z o.o., Wrocław